Do better if possible, and that is always possible
FRANÇOIS CONSTANTIN – 1819

EDITORIAL MANAGEMENT
Suzanne Tise-Isoré
Collection Style et Design

PUBLICATION MANAGER AT VACHERON CONSTANTIN
Anne-Marie Bubanko Belcari

COORDINATION AT VACHERON CONSTANTIN
Caroline Quiniou

EDITORIAL ASSISTANCE
Sarah Rozelle
Boris Guilbert

ART DIRECTION
Pitis e Associati, Paris

COPYEDITING AND PROOFREADING
Barbara Mellor

PRODUCTION
Corinne Trovarelli

COLOR SEPARATION
Les Artisans du Regard, Paris

PRINTING BY
Musumeci S.p.A., Italy

Simultaneously published in French as
Vacheron Constantin Référence 57260
© Flammarion, S.A., Paris, 2016
© Vacheron Constantin, 2016

English-language edition
© Flammarion, S.A., Paris, 2016
© Vacheron Constantin, 2016

editions.flammarion.com
styleetdesign-flammarion.com

16 17 18   3 2 1
ISBN: 978-2-08-020275-8
Legal Deposit: 04/2017

VACHERON CONSTANTIN
REFERENCE 57260

Flammarion

CONTENTS

Do better if possible, and that is always possible.
FRANÇOIS CONSTANTIN – 1819

Ever since its creation over 260 years ago, Vacheron Constantin has consistently cultivated privileged ties with its clients, and provided its watchmakers with opportunities to create bespoke watches. We do everything in our power to infuse a watch with the character that will enduringly reflect the choices made by its owner, while ensuring respect for the values of the Maison and for the art of fine watchmaking.

In the eighteenth century, prestigious clients were accustomed to placing orders with *cabinotiers*, the watchmaking artisans who forged Geneva's reputation. This tradition has remained firmly in place within the Maison. From Tsar Alexander II to New York banker Henry Graves Jr, from automobile manufacturer James Ward Packard to King Fuad I and King Farouk of Egypt, many distinguished figures have been major collectors of the one-of-a-kind models created by Vacheron Constantin.

The Manufacture has thus made bespoke watches since 1755 and has accordingly created a department specifically dedicated to this activity, Les Cabinotiers, which perpetuates the distinctive Geneva spirit inherited from the Age of Enlightenment.

Timepieces from the Cabinotiers department evolve from a privileged relationship with the individuals who order them. Above and beyond the product itself, this is a highly exclusive service based on listening to clients' wishes and requirements, as well as on continuous exchanges with the watchmakers, spanning the entire process, from design and development through to the production of each individual timepiece.

The Reference 57260 watch perfectly epitomizes these exchanges between Vacheron Constantin and a passionately dedicated collector.

This horological masterpiece with two faces is distinguished by its scarcely conceivable complexity and technical innovation. Developed and crafted by three of our master watchmakers, it required eight full years of development, and naturally bears the prestigious Hallmark of Geneva.

Through its combination of traditional watchmaking principles with technical advances, the Reference 57260 watch comprises 57 complications, several of which are world firsts, such as the double retrograde split-second chronograph, as well as a number of calendars, including a perpetual Hebrew calendar unique in watchmaking. It was therefore only natural to devote a part of this publication to these "recorders of time".

Presented in 2015, the 260th anniversary of the founding of Vacheron Constantin, this exceptional model perpetuates the line of unique creations that have punctuated its history, many of them born of a similarly privileged meeting between a distinguished patron and the genius of an artist from a great Maison.

Featuring a new chapter in the history of the oldest Manufacture without interruption since 1755, this masterpiece will forever mark the conquest of time, as undertaken by man since his origins.

— *Juan Carlos Torres*
CEO Vacheron Constantin

CHAPTER 1

THE PROUD TRADITION
OF GRAND COMPLICATIONS

The special ties that the Maison Vacheron Constantin cultivates with its clients, all discerning devotees of exceptional and personalized objects, have been cultivated since 1755. Passionate collectors are keenly aware of this privilege, as are enlightened connoisseurs.

Today, the Cabinotiers department of the Manufacture embodies the watchmaking spirit of the eighteenth-century city of Geneva by offering this unique and unprecedented service dedicated to Fine Watchmaking.

The dialogue between the patron who commissioned the Reference 57260 and the Vacheron Constantin master watchmakers led to unprecedented, in-depth research that has significantly contributed to the advancement of horological and mechanical science.

This one-of-a-kind creation belongs to a proud lineage demonstrating impressive credentials in the fields of precision, technical mastery and inspired aesthetics.

Through a selection of these timepieces from its Heritage collection, Vacheron Constantin invites readers to journey through time, and thereby confirms its expertise and its constant pursuit of excellence.

Facing page The two faces of Reference 57260, the world's most complicated watch.

1827

POCKET WATCH WITH STRIKING COMPLICATIONS

Elegant early nineteenth-century watch featuring a simplicity and legibility that make it a perfect example of the style in vogue at the time.

DESCRIPTION

Pocket watch with *guilloché* rose gold case. | *Guilloché* silver dial with black enameled Roman numerals, peripheral minutes circle with markers and five-minute dots, rose gold hands. | Key winding. | Cylinder escapement. | Dimensions: 62 mm in diameter, 17 mm thick. | Inventory no. 10715.

FUNCTIONS

This watch with striking complications is equipped with a grande sonnerie, a petite sonnerie and a quarter repeater function.

1905

POCKET WATCH WITH
TEN COMPLICATIONS

Its multiple functions meant that this type
of timepiece was referred to at the time
as an explorer's watch.

DESCRIPTION

Pocket watch with 18K yellow gold case. | Enamel dial with Arabic numerals, peripheral minutes circle with red Arabic numerals for five-minute intervals, small seconds at 6 o'clock, hands in gold and blued steel. | Pendant-set winding. | Lever escapement. | Bimetallic cut balance wheel, balance-spring with overcoil, swan's neck regulator with micrometer screw. | Dimensions: 51 mm in diameter, 17 mm thick. | Vacheron Constantin Heritage collection. | Inventory no. 10158.

FUNCTIONS

This watch is equipped with a split-seconds chronograph and a 30-minute counter at 12 o'clock, as well as a minute repeater striking on two gongs. | Its 48-month perpetual calendar represents the four-year cycle: date at 3 o'clock, days of the week at 9 o'clock, indication of the current year within the leap-year cycle at 12 o'clock. | Phases and age of the moon at 6 o'clock.

1917

POCKET WATCH WITH
EIGHT COMPLICATIONS

The Vacheron Constantin archives observe of this watch: *"Finissage 19', verre RC QP et phase de Lune, 4 remises, équation, lever et coucher du soleil d'après Paris. … mise à l'heure par tirage"*, an example of the kind of technical description provided at the time.

DESCRIPTION

Pocket watch with 18K yellow gold case. | Enamel dial with Arabic numerals, peripheral railway-track minute circle, small seconds at 6 o'clock, blued steel hands. A gold hand tipped with a sun indicates the Equation of time. | Pendant-set winding. | Dimensions: 19''' caliber (42.8 mm). | Model 1067.

FUNCTIONS

This watch with astronomical functions features a perpetual calendar (days of the week and date at 6 o'clock, months and moon phases at 12 o'clock) and a running equation of time complemented by sunrise and sunset times in Paris at 9 and 3 o'clock respectively.

1918

POCKET WATCH WITH
SEVEN COMPLICATIONS

*personalized and delivered
to James Ward Packard*

This watch was created and personalized for James Ward Packard (1863–1928), the American industrial magnate who founded the Packard Motor Company, an enlightened collector of highly complicated horology.

DESCRIPTION

Pocket watch with 20K gold case adorned with a finely chased floral motif on the case middle, bezel and pendant. | Its back features a *JWP* monogram set in a triangular cartouche surrounded by an Art Deco style frame in champlevé blue enamel against a finely chased background. | Enamel dial with Roman hours numerals, peripheral railway-track minutes circle with Arabic numerals marking five-minute intervals, small seconds at 6 o'clock, blued steel hands. | Pendant-set winding. | Lever escapement. | Guillaume balance wheel. | Movement with two barrels: one for the going train of the watch and the other for the striking mechanisms. | Dimensions: 57 mm in diameter, 18 mm thick. | Vacheron Constantin Heritage collection. | Inventory no. 11527.

FUNCTIONS

This watch is endowed with a 30-minute chronograph counter at 12 o'clock. | Its audible functions comprise a grande sonnerie, petite sonnerie, quarter repeater, half-quarter repeater and silence function.

Sir Bhupindra Singh, Maharaja
of Patiala (1913–1974).

1921

POCKET WATCH WITH SIX COMPLICATIONS

sold to the Maharaja of Patiala

This pocket watch certified by the Geneva Observatory was acquired among other models by Sir Bhupindra Singh, Maharaja of Patiala, a gifted sportsman, generous humanitarian and keen collector of jewelry watches.

DESCRIPTION

Pocket watch with 18K yellow gold case. | Finely grained matt silver-toned dial, Roman hour numerals, peripheral minutes circle with Arabic numerals marking every five minutes, blued steel hands. Two gold hands indicating the date and day. | Pendant-set winding and alarm slide-piece at 9 o'clock. | Dimensions: 60 mm in diameter, 18 mm thick. | Vacheron Constantin Heritage collection. | Inventory no. 10156.

FUNCTIONS

This watch associated with the world of travel is equipped with a chronograph function featuring a 15-minute counter at 12 o'clock, a simple calendar showing the days of the week at 9 o'clock and the date at 3 o'clock, along with moon phases at 6 o'clock and an alarm function in the center.

1929

POCKET WATCH WITH THIRTEEN COMPLICATIONS

presented to Fuad I of Egypt

An exceptional watch chosen by Francis Peter, a Swiss citizen, judge and President of the Mixed Court of Cairo, as a gift from the Swiss colony in Egypt to King Fuad I of Egypt, a discerning connoisseur and reputed collector of Fine Watchmaking. It was also exhibited that same year at the World's Fair in Barcelona.

DESCRIPTION

Pocket watch with 18K yellow gold case, adorned on the back with the royal insignia of Egypt crafted using Geneva enameling techniques. | Grained-finish silver dial with Arabic numerals, peripheral railway-track minutes circle with Arabic numerals for five-minute intervals, small seconds at 6 o'clock, blued steel hands. | Pendant winding. | Lever escapement. | Bimetallic cut balance wheel, balance spring with overcoil, swan's neck regulator with micrometer screw | Movement with two barrels: one for the going train of the watch, and the other to supply the energy required for the striking mechanisms. | Dimensions: 65 mm in diameter, 25 mm thick. | Private collection.

FUNCTIONS

This model is equipped with a split-seconds chronograph featuring a 30-minute counter at 3 o'clock. | The grande sonnerie, petite sonnerie and minute repeater are struck on three gongs, complemented by a silence function. | Its 12-month perpetual calendar depicts the four-year cycle with the indication of the current year within the leap-year cycle at 9 o'clock. Days of the week and date through an aperture at 12 o'clock. | Phases and age of the moon at 6 o'clock.

Chronomètre-chronographe avec sonnerie à 2 carillons et calendrier perpétuel montrant également les phases de la lune, offert à S. M. le Roi Fouad par la Colonie suisse d'Egypte.

CHRONOMÈTRE OFFERT PAR LA COLONIE SUISSE D'EGYPTE A SA MAJESTÉ FOUAD Ier, ROI D'EGYPTE

Ce chronomètre comporte toutes les principales complications, soit *Chronographe* au cinquième de seconde avec dédoublante et rattrapante, compteur de *minutes*.

Répétition. La montre sonne à volonté les heures, les quarts et les minutes, les quarts formant carillon sur trois timbres.

Grande et petite sonnerie. On entend par *grande sonnerie* le fait que, telle une pendule, la montre sonne d'elle-même en passant les heures et les quarts. *La petite sonnerie* permet de ne faire sonner en passant que les quarts seulement. Le tout peut d'ailleurs être arrêté à volonté par l'un des verrous sur la carrure de la montre.

Quantième perpétuel avec indication des mois par une aiguille spéciale dans le petit cadran de gauche. Celui-ci est divisé en quatre années, l'autre petite aiguille en forme de flèche indiquant s'il s'agit d'une année ordinaire ou d'une année bissextile. Cette petite aiguille fait donc un seul tour de cadran en quatre ans. Sous le guichet apparaissent les jours de la semaine et les quantièmes du mois. Ce quantième qui, dans les années ordinaire saute du 28 février au 1er mars, indique de lui-même le 29 février les années bissextiles.

Enfin, le petit cadran du bas comporte en premier lieu l'aiguille des secondes habituelle. En plus, sous le guichet, apparaissent *les phases de lune.* L'on remarquera la numérotation spéciale de ce cadran qui, outre les secondes de 5 en 5, porte aussi les *chiffres zéro* et 29 ½ représentant la période des lunaisons.

Cette pièce, qui constitue un des plus beaux exemplaires de la Chronométrie suisse, est logé dans un boîtier extra fort en or 18 carats dont le fond est décoré des Armoiries Royales en émail, travail d'une grande finesse dû à l'un des premiers artistes de Genève.

Coffret. Coffret en palissandre avec panneaux en loupe d'amboine, avec sur le couvercle la couronne royale et le chiffre arabe de S. M. en or incrusté. Intérieurement, la date 1929 en gravure sur or incrusté entouré de deux écussons peinture sur émail, l'un étant l'écusson suisse, l'autre les armoiries royales.

Presentation article, 1929.
Vacheron Constantin Heritage Archives.

King Fuad I of Egypt
(1868–1936).

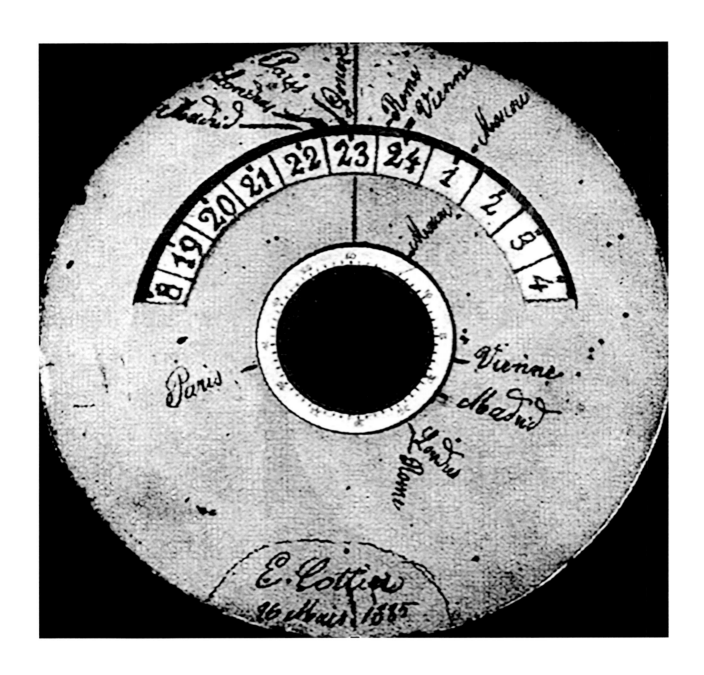

1885 drawing, presented by Emmanuel
Cottier (1858–1930), father of Louis
Cottier and former Vacheron Constantin
watchmaker, following the adoption of the
24 time zones at the International Meridian
Conference held in Washington in 1884.
Musée d'Art et d'Histoire, Geneva.

1932

WORLD TIME
POCKET WATCH

based on the Louis Cottier principle

The first watch made in 1932 and bearing the Vacheron Constantin signature to feature the World Time system developed by Louis Cottier, a watchmaker based in Carouge near Geneva (1894–1966), followed on from the early work conducted in this field by his father Emmanuel in 1885.

DESCRIPTION

Pocket watch with an 18K rose gold case middle, white gold bezel and back, rose gold slanted-edged pendant. | Central chapter ring of hour-markers, rose beaded minute circle, polished steel hands. | Pendant-set winding. | Lever escapement. | Dimensions: 45 mm in diameter. | Model 3372.

FUNCTIONS

The fixed outer dial ring bears the name of 31 of the world's cities and sites: Berlin, Rome, Cape Town, Istanbul, Cairo, Aden, Mauritius, Mumbai, Kolkata, Singapore, Beijing, Albany, Tokyo, Sydney, Auckland, Fiji, Hawaii, Alaska, Klondike, Vancouver, San Francisco, Denver, Chicago, Montreal, New York, Buenos Aires, Rio de Janeiro, the Azores, Madeira, London and Paris. | The 24 time zones are read by rotating the 24-hour disc and positioning the triangular markers pointing to the 31 cities. | The main time-zone indication at 12 o'clock was determined by the customer, who chose the reference city when ordering the watch.

1932

WATCH WITH
ELEVEN COMPLICATIONS

Winner of the first prize in the 1934 Geneva
Observatory competition, a reliable token of excellence
in the realm of chronometry (precision timing).

DESCRIPTION

Pocket with 18K yellow gold case. | Grained-finish silver-toned dial with Arabic numerals,
peripheral railway-track minutes circle with Arabic numerals marking five-minute intervals, small
seconds at 6 o'clock, blued steel hands. | Pendant-set winding. | Tourbillon 60 seconds with Guillaume
balance wheel. | Dimensions: 66 mm in diameter, 22 mm thick. | Vacheron Constantin Heritage
collection. | Inventory no. 10951.

FUNCTIONS

This watch is equipped with a split-seconds chronograph featuring a 30-minute counter
at 12 o'clock. | Its 48-month perpetual calendar displays the four-year cycle: date at 3 o'clock, months
at 6 o'clock, days of the week at 9 o'clock and indication of the current year within the leap-year cycle
at 12 o'clock. | Phases and age of the moon at 6 o'clock. | Power-reserve indicator at 12 o'clock.

1936

MEN'S WRISTWATCH
WITH FOUR COMPLICATIONS,
BARREL-SHAPED WATCH

REFERENCE 57260

The *tonneau* (barrel) shape first appeared around 1990
and combines curves and straight lines, so giving
dialmakers ample space to express their talent.

DESCRIPTION

Men's wristwatch, 18K yellow gold barrel-shaped case. | Silver-toned dial, blue Arabic numerals,
peripheral railway-type minutes circle, small seconds at 6 o'clock, blued steel hands. | Winding via
the crown positioned at 12 o'clock between the two case lugs. | Lever escapement. | Dimensions:
11''' caliber (24.8 mm). | Model 3620.

FUNCTIONS

This watch is equipped with a minute repeater. Its perpetual calendar indicates the date by means
of a central retrograde hand and the days of the week on a pointer-type display at 6 o'clock, but does not
show the month.

1946

POCKET WATCH WITH
FIFTEEN COMPLICATIONS

made for King Farouk of Egypt

Watch intended for King Farouk of Egypt and delivered
in 1946 to His Excellency Bulent Rauf (1911–1987),
husband of the sovereign's sister, Princess Faiza.

DESCRIPTION

Large 18K yellow gold pocket watch, gilt metal dial, Arabic numerals, peripheral railway-track minutes circle with Arabic numerals marking five-minute intervals, small seconds at 6 o'clock, blued steel hands, gold alarm hand. | Pendant-set winding. | Movement with three barrels: one for the going train of the watch, and the other to supply the energy required for the striking mechanisms. | Dimensions: 85 mm in diameter, 26 mm thick. | Private collection.

FUNCTIONS

This exceptional watch features a split-seconds chronograph featuring a 30-minute counter at 3 o'clock. | Grande sonnerie, petite sonnerie and minute repeater on three gongs, complemented by a silence function and an alarm. | The 12-month perpetual calendar is complemented by the days of the week at 9 o'clock, the date at 6 o'clock, and the indication of the present year within the leap-year cycle at 12 o'clock. | Phases of the moon at 6 o'clock. | Power-reserve indicators at 3 o'clock for the movement and at 9 o'clock for the striking mechanism torque.

King Farouk of Egypt (1920–1965).

1948

POCKET WATCH WITH TEN COMPLICATIONS

delivered to Count Guy de Boisrouvray

Exceptional model delivered to Count Guy
de Boisrouvray, first cousin of Prince Rainier III
of Monaco, keen connoisseur and collector
of historical paintings and works of applied art.

DESCRIPTION

Pocket watch with hunter-type case in 18K yellow gold. | Silver-toned dial with Arabic numerals,
peripheral "railway-track" minute circle with Arabic numerals marking five-minute intervals, small
seconds at 6 o'clock, blued steel hands. A gold hand indicates the alarm time. | Pendant-set winding
for the movement and the alarm. | Movement with three barrels. | Lever escapement. | Guillaume
balance wheel. | Dimensions: 67 mm in diameter, 20 mm thick. | Private collection.

FUNCTIONS

This model is equipped with a split-seconds chronograph featuring a 30-minute counter
at 12 o'clock. | The three minute-repeater hammers strike a set of three gongs. | Its 48-month perpetual
calendar depicts the four-year cycle: date at 6 o'clock, days of the week at 9 o'clock, months and
indication of the current year within the leap-year cycle at 3 o'clock. | Phases of the moon
at 12 o'clock. | Alarm.

1964

POCKET WATCH WITH
TEN COMPLICATIONS

REFERENCE 57260

The elegance of this watch, accentuated by its arch-shaped pendant, gives a modern accent to a multifunction dial that is both classic and timeless.

DESCRIPTION

Pocket watch with case in 18K yellow gold. | Silver-toned dial, hours indicated by yellow gold baton-type hour-markers, peripheral railway-track minutes circle with Arabic numerals marking five-minute intervals, gold and blued steel hands. | Pendant-set winding. | Lever escapement. | Dimensions: 52 mm in diameter, 12 mm thick, 17''' caliber. | Vacheron Constantin Heritage collection. | Inventory no. 11698.

FUNCTIONS

This watch is equipped with a split-seconds chronograph featuring a 30-minute counter at 12 o'clock and a minute repeater. | Its 48-month perpetual calendar depicts the four-year cycle: date at 3 o'clock, months at 6 o'clock, days of the week at 9 o'clock, indication of the current month and year within the leap-year cycle at 12 o'clock. | Phases and age of the moon at 6 o'clock.

2005

COMMEMORATIVE WATCH
WITH SIXTEEN COMPLICATIONS
ON A TWIN-FACED DISPLAY

LA TOUR DE L'ÎLE

Historical model developed and issued as a seven-piece limited edition in 2005, to commemorate the 250th anniversary of the founding of Maison Vacheron Constantin. Its name pays tribute to the place where Vacheron Constantin installed its workshops in the early 1840s. Equipped with sixteen complications, it represented a world first at the time.

DESCRIPTION

Men's wristwatch with an 18K rose gold case. | Main dial on the front in silver-toned, hand-*guilloché* yellow gold, 18K rose gold applied Roman numerals, peripheral minutes circle with Arabic numerals marking the five-minute intervals. | Gold hours and minutes hands inspired by a 1926 model and blued steel hands. Small seconds fitted to the tourbillon arbor at 6 o'clock. | Back dial in silver-toned 18K yellow gold, hand-*guilloché* with an exclusive motif. | Manual crown winding. | 60-second tourbillon with lever escapement, placed at 6 o'clock and featuring a carriage shaped like the Maltese cross brand emblem. | Hand-engraved applied gold the Hallmark of Geneva at 4 o'clock on the dial. | Dimensions: 47 mm in diameter, 18 mm thick. | Vacheron Constantin Heritage collection. | Inventory no. 11474.

FUNCTIONS

The watch is equipped with a minute repeater and a tourbillon bearing the seconds function.

MAIN DIAL ON THE FRONT

Indicator of the striking mechanism torque – the state of wind of the minute repeater mechanism at 1 o'clock. | Phases and age of the moon at 3 o'clock. | Seconds at 6 o'clock. | Power-reserve indicator at 9 o'clock. | Dual-time display at 11 o'clock, with day/night indication.

BACK DIAL

12-month perpetual calendar: date at 3 o'clock, days of the week at 9 o'clock, months at 12 o'clock. | Indication of the current year within the leap-year cycle through an aperture at 2 o'clock. | Perpetual equation of time on a sector in the center. | Sunrise and sunset times, calculated for the latitude and longitude of Geneva, appearing on sectors positioned respectively at 8 and 4 o'clock. | Accurate, real-time sky chart of the northern hemisphere at 6 o'clock.

2010

WRISTWATCH WITH
THREE COMPLICATIONS

|

PHILOSOPHIA
delivered to the collector who commissioned it

The name of this model, given by the collector who commissioned this watch with its distinctive display, implies that human beings do not need to know the time to the nearest minute. Time is indeed a realm of sempiternal thought that has been evoked throughout the history of philosophy.

DESCRIPTION

Men's wristwatch with an 18K rose gold case, of which the back is engraved with the inscription *Les Cabinotiers*, the *AC* – Ateliers Cabinotiers – insignia and the Hallmark of Geneva. | Opaline silver-toned 24-hour dial, Arabic numerals from 2 to 24 for the even-numbered hours, dots for the odd-numbered hours, minutes sounded by the minute repeater rather than displayed. | Blued steel hours hand, gold seconds hand fitted on the tourbillon arbor. | Manual crown winding. | 60-second tourbillon with lever escapement, placed at 6 o'clock and featuring a carriage shaped like the Maltese cross brand emblem. | Hand-engraved rose gold moon. | The Hallmark of Geneva. | Dimensions: case 43 mm in diameter, movement 33 mm in diameter, movement 8 mm thick. | One-of-a-kind model, private collection.

FUNCTIONS

The watch is equipped with a minute repeater and a tourbillon displaying the seconds. | Phases of the moon at 9 o'clock. | The power-reserve indicator on the back is enhanced with a plate bearing the Big and Little Dipper constellations entwined.

2012

WRISTWATCH WITH SEVENTEEN COMPLICATIONS ON A TWIN-FACED DISPLAY

VLADIMIR

The name Vladimir given by the collector who commissioned this one-of-a-kind watch is derived from the ancient name Volodymyr, meaning "possessor of the world" or "peace upon all".

DESCRIPTION

Men's wristwatch. 18K rose gold case featuring the twelve signs of the Chinese zodiac engraved on its middle. | 18K white gold hand-*guilloché* dial, Arabic numerals, peripheral minutes circle with Arabic numerals marking the five-minute intervals. Dauphine-type gold hands and blued steel hands, small seconds fitted on the tourbillon arbor. | Manual crown winding. | 60-second tourbillon with lever escapement, placed at 6 o'clock and featuring a carriage shaped like the Vacheron Constantin Maltese cross brand emblem. | The Hallmark of Geneva. | Dimensions: 47 mm in diameter. | One-of-a-kind model, private collection.

FUNCTIONS

The watch is equipped with a minute repeater and with a tourbillon bearing the seconds display.

MAIN FRONT DIAL

Power-reserve indicator at 1 o'clock. | Week number and indicator of the striking mechanism torque – the state of wind of the minute repeater – at 9 o'clock. | Dual-time display with day/night indicator at 11 o'clock. | Phases and age of the moon at 3 o'clock.

BACK DIAL

12-month perpetual calendar: date at 2 o'clock, days of the week at 10 o'clock, months at 12 o'clock. | Indication of the current year within the leap-year cycle at 1 o'clock. | Equation of time on a sector in the center. | Sunrise and sunrise times, calculated for the latitude and longitude of Moscow, displayed on sectors at 8 and 4 o'clock respectively. | Accurate sky chart of the northern hemisphere at 6 o'clock.

2014

WRISTWATCH WITH
FIFTEEN COMPLICATIONS
ON A TWIN-FACED DISPLAY

MAÎTRE CABINOTIER
ASTRONOMICA

Inspired by the Tour de l'Île model, this one-of-a-kind creation displays – among much other information – astronomical data rarely provided by a wristwatch, such as the zodiac signs, seasons, solstices and equinoxes.

DESCRIPTION

Men's wristwatch, 18K white gold case, opaline slate-grey white gold dial, 18K white gold applied hour-markers, peripheral railway-track minutes circle, white gold hands, small seconds hand on the tourbillon carriage at 6 o'clock. | Manual crown winding. | 60-second tourbillon with lever escapement placed at 6 o'clock and featuring a carriage shaped like the Maltese cross brand emblem. | The Hallmark of Geneva. | Dimensions: 47 mm in diameter, 19 mm thick. | One-of-a-kind model, private collection.

FUNCTIONS

The watch is equipped with a minute repeater featuring an ingenious centripetal strike governor and a tourbillon serving to display the seconds.

MAIN DIAL ON THE FRONT

12-month perpetual calendar calculated for 400 years; date between 2 and 3 o'clock; days of the week between 9 and 10 o'clock; months at 12 o'clock. | Indication of the current year within the leap-year cycle through an aperture at 1 o'clock. | Power-reserve indication on a sector at 9 o'clock. | Equation of time on a sector at 11 o'clock. | Sunrise and sunset times, calculated for the latitude and longitude of a reference location chosen by the collector who commissioned the watch, appearing on sectors at 8 and 4 o'clock respectively.

BACK DIAL

Sky chart viewed from the northern hemisphere with four cardinal points in the center. | Displays of the months of the sidereal year in the south and of sidereal time in the north. The latter enables the watchmakers to position the sky chart according to the chosen reference time. | The hand tipped with a sun points to the zodiac sign, the date of the month, the season, the equinox or the solstice closest to the current date; while the one without a sun points to the phases and age of the moon.

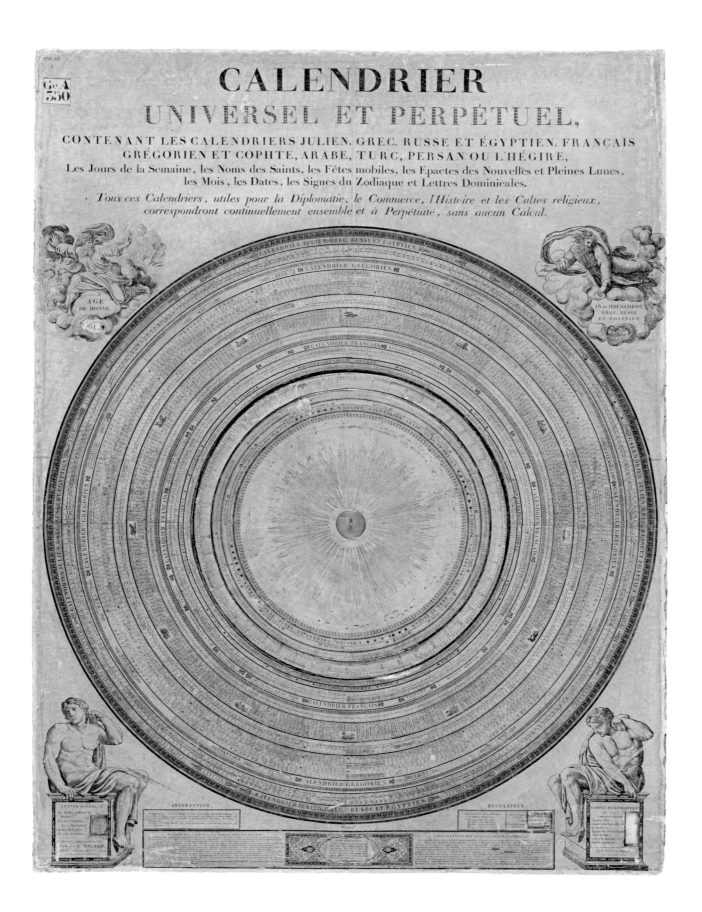

CHAPTER 2

THE CALENDAR: RECORDER OF TIME

Two heavenly bodies govern the path
of the earth and determine the timespans
that will form the basis of any calendar.

The *day* – one daytime period followed by one night – is the time that elapses between two risings or settings of the sun, or else between two of its passages through the meridian, the imaginary circle spanning through the earth's two poles. The *month* is the time that elapses between two consecutive full moons. Finally, the *year*, like the day, is governed by the sun, and ends when the latter returns to the same given point in the sky. Thus these two heavenly bodies that light our existence by night and by day, immutable and indispensable presences that have always been the twin focus of symbolism and science, set the pace of our lives on earth.

Facing page Universal and perpetual calendar containing the Julian, Greek, French and Russian, Gregorian and Coptic, Arab, Turkish, Persian and Hegira calendars, as well as moveable feast days, epacts, months, dates, signs of the Zodiac and dominical letters. Invented and made by J.-A. Richard in Paris in 1806.

THE INVENTION OF THE CALENDAR
& THE ESTABLISHMENT
OF THE RHYTHMS OF TIME

Charting the memory of history, the calendar is the ultimate archive. It is the benchmark of the chronology of history, the tool by which both science and the arts seek to understand the transformation of the world. The invention of the calendar as the recorder of time was no hasty or improvised matter, but stemmed instead from an extremely lengthy process progressing from ever more refined methods of observation to mature analysis. An invention can only be validated through acceptance and use. In the context of the apparent regularity of repeated cycles of time, ancient observations of the paths of the sun, the moon and the constellations noted irregularities that were themselves repeated. As these observations became steadily more acute, subtle variations were discovered and recorded. Humankind adopted two key methods of understanding and preserving the memory of the rhythms of nature: counting and using signs to record observations. Counting evolved into calculations, and signs into writing.

Facing page *A scribe, a mathematician and an astrologist holding an astrolabe. Psalter of Saint Louis and Blanche de Castile, thirteenth century. Illuminated manuscript on parchment.*

Without these two skills, human beings could not master the world in which they lived. By setting out to deduce how the time spans ordained by heavenly bodies were organized, they became cartographers and horologists.

Mesopotamia – the vast plain watered by the majestic Tigris and Euphrates that corresponds more or less to modern-day Iraq – was the cradle of one of the most ancient and remarkable civilizations on earth. It is to Chaldea in southern Mesopotamia, also called the kingdom of Sumer, with its influential cities of Ur and later Babylon, that we owe the development of cuneiform script and the first transcriptions of astronomical observations, dating back to around 3500 BCE. The vast, clear Mesopotamian night sky was a perfect backdrop for observing the stars. The origins of calendar calculations are to be found here. It was the Chaldeans and subsequently the Assyrians who first used the sexagesimal (base 60) number system, although its exact development is somewhat obscure. The Greek historian Herodotus (c.484-420 BCE) indicated that the Chaldeans divided days into ten hours as well as into sixtieths. Later, the mathematician Theon of Alexandria (335-405 BCE), commenting on the writings of the Egyptian astronomer Ptolemy (who died in 168 BCE), claimed that the number 60 was chosen because it was the lowest common multiple of 1, 2, 3, 4, 5, and 6. The decision to divide the circle into 360 degrees, meanwhile, may relate to the apparent annual motion of the earth, which takes around 360 days to realign with the same stars in the same positions.

TO EACH CIVILIZATION
ITS CALENDAR

Myths and rites are our way of counting out the days of our existence, a legacy and a heritage for succeeding generations, carefully preserved to mark out the infinite course of human history. While feast days broke up this rhythm or marked out specific periods, often on an annual basis, they were first and foremost opportunities for gatherings and meetings: with nature, with the sacred, with other people, with oneself. They became both

milestones and footprints, combining religion, culture, and worship with the political and economic activities that together make up a society. The complexity of their raison d'être, their meaning and their repercussions is a common feature of all civilizations. Every feast day or holy day – whatever its significance to a particular group of people in a particular calendar – is deeply enmeshed in this web of interlocking meanings.

Facing page The month of February,
illumination from the *Très Riches Heures
du duc de Berry*, Limbourg brothers, 1411–16.

Above October.

Above, right June.

Right July.

THE CHINESE CALENDAR

For the Chinese, the calendar is the receptacle of a universal harmony bringing together the different dimensions of earth, heaven, and humankind. The sounds and flavors of nature, the seasons, work days and feast days, and the course of the moon all play their part this harmony. The lunisolar Chinese calendar comprises twelve lunar months: the first day of the month is the new moon, and the fifteenth day is the full moon. To compensate for the ten days of the solar year missing from the lunar year, seven months are intercalated into a nineteen-year cycle. This means that the Chinese calendar year is as close as possible to the rhythm of the sun. The best-known and most sophisticated Chinese calendar is that introduced by the Emperor Han Wu-Ti, around 104 CE, which continued in use for over twenty centuries. The use of this traditional calendar was officially abolished in 1912, but the Gregorian calendar was not adopted by the nation as a whole until 1929.

To the Chinese, astrology played an indispensable role in the functioning of the world, and the "science" of prediction formed an integral part of each annual calendar. The emperor would set up a special committee composed of equal numbers of astronomers and astrologists. Together, and with the help of accurate measuring instruments inspired by celestial calculations, they would draw up the agenda for the administrative tasks of the year. Adhering to the imperial calendar was a sign of loyalty, departing from it a token of rebellion. For agricultural tasks,

EARTHLY BRANCHES	LUNAR MONTHS	CARDINAL POINTS	SEASON OR "KNOT"	HOURS OF THE DAY	ANIMAL
1 Tzu	11	N	Winter	11 to 13	Rat
2 Tch'ou	12	N NE		13 to 15	Ox
3 Yin	1	E NE		15 to 17	Tiger
4 Mao	2	E	Spring	17 to 19	Hare
5 Tch'en	3	E SE		19 to 21	Dragon
6 Ssu	4	S SE		21 to 23	Snake
7 Wu	5	S	Summer	23 to 01	Horse
8 Wei	6	S SW		1 to 3	Sheep
9 Shen	7	W SW		3 to 5	Monkey
10 Yu	8	W	Autumn	5 to 7	Rooster
11 Hsü	9	W NW		7 to 9	Dog
12 Haï	10	N NW		9 to 11	Pig

Table inspired by Louis Molet
in *"Comput et Calendriers, Histoire
des Mœurs"*, *Encyclopédie de la Pléiade*,
Éditions Gallimard, Paris 1990.

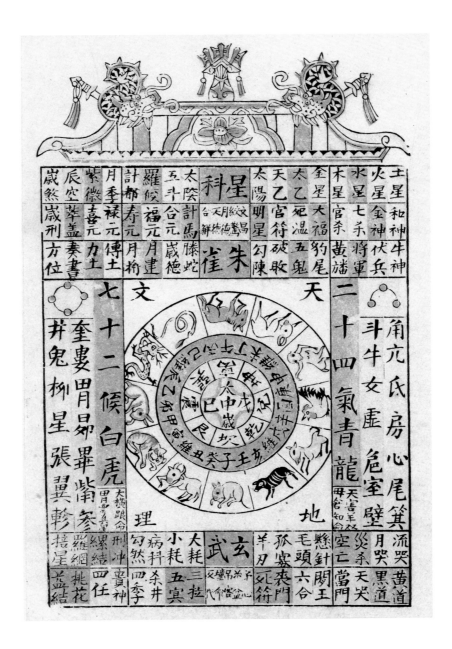

the Chinese used a succession of twenty-four periods of about fifteen days, each described as either a knot (*jie*) or a breath (*qi*). Each knot or breath was given a name denoting a season, a quality of air or light, a stage in germination, or some other aspect of the farming year. It was a tool that was as poetic as it was valuable for the accomplishment of seasonal tasks.

The Chinese calendar used a number of different cycles, including nineteen- and seventy-six-year variations. And there was also a sixty-day cycle, divided into combinations of six times ten "heavenly boughs" and twelve "earthly branches". Within this cycle, the day was composed of twelve equal two-hour sections. The Chinese made a link between the twelve earthly branches and the lunar months, the cardinal points, the seasons, the hours of the day, and animals.

Above *Heavenly stems and earthly branches.* Heavenly stems are a Chinese concept relating to the sexagesimal cycle: there are ten of them and they are associated with Yin-Yang and the five elements. The twelve earthly branches are associated with the twelve animals of the Chinese Zodiac. Qing dynasty, preserved in the National Museum of History, Taipei.

Pages 46–47 Thirteenth century Tibetan manuscript depicting the twelve signs of the Chinese zodiac.

45

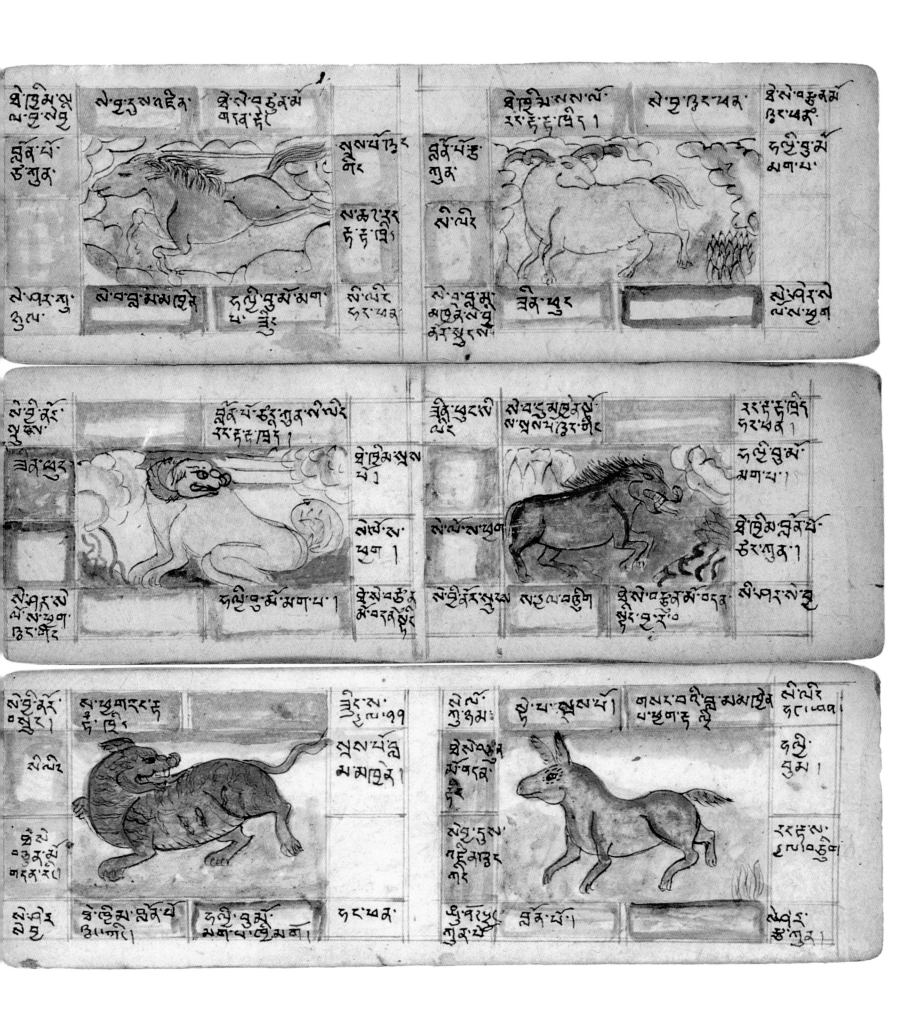

THE ISLAMIC CALENDAR

Islam is followed by hundreds of millions of Muslims across the world, and especially in the countries of Asia and Africa. Some countries, including Sadi Arabia, Yemen and the United Arab Emirates, have adopted the Islamic calendar as their official calendar. While there are differences in the celebration of certain feast days in specific cultures, the basic calendar is the same for all Muslims.

MUSLIM MONTHS	NUMBER OF DAYS
1 Muharram	30
2 Safar	29
3 Rabi' al-awwal	30
4 Rabi' al-tháni	29
5 Djumadá al-awwal	30
6 Djumadá al-thani	29
7 Radjab	30
8 Cha'ban	29
9 Ramadan	30
10 Chawwal	29
11 Dhu'al-qa'da	30
12 Dhu'al-hidjdja	29 or 30

The prescriptions laid down by the Prophet Muhammad (Mecca, 570 – Medina, 632 CE), as the representative of Allah, were transcribed by his disciples and brought together in the Qu'ran, in the form of 114 chapters or Surahs. The Muslim era begins on September 22 or 23, 622 CE, date of the Hegira, marking Muhammad's journey from Mecca to Medina. The official Islamic calendar was established in year 16 of the Hegira (638 CE) by the caliph Omar.

Muslim religious practice is founded on five mandatory principles: a profession of faith in one god, Allah, and in his prophet Muhammad; daily prayers repeated five times; a ritual purifying tax in the form of alms; continuous daytime fasting during the month of Ramadan; and a pilgrimage to Mecca once in a lifetime. Friday is the holy day, devoted to solemn prayer. The Muslim devotional year is punctuated by two types of celebrations: those relating to the life of the Prophet, and those relating to the calendar. These fall on different dates according to Sunni, Shiite and Sufi beliefs. The three most important are: the beginning of the Islamic new year, on the first day of the month of Muharram; the celbrations marking the end the month-long fast of Ramadan, Eid al-Fitr; and the sacrificial feast of Eid al-Adha commemorating Ibrahim's willingness to sacrifice his son and the angelic vision that commanded him to sacrifice a sheep instead.

Facing page Fourteenth-century gouache depicting the divisions of the year, from *Marvels of Creatures and the Strange Things Existing*, by Al-Qazwini.

Exclusively lunar, the Islamic calendar is based on the Qu'ran (Surah 9.36): "Indeed, the number of months with Allah is twelve [lunar] months in the register of Allah [from] the day He created the heavens and the earth." The number of days in a month is thirty or twenty-nine, in regular alternation. The Muslim year lasts 354 days, making a discrepancy of eleven and a quarter days from the Gregorian year. The lunar equation of time carries a forty-four-minute difference between the true lunar cycle and the mean lunar cycle. This is compensated by

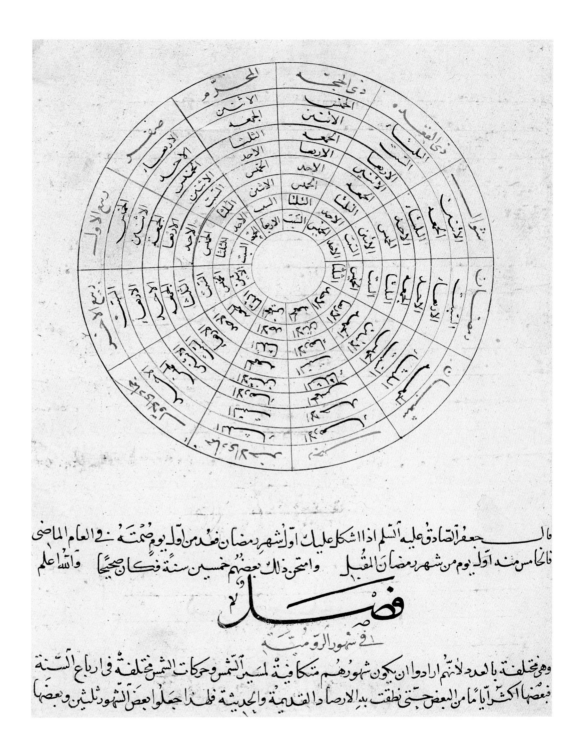

adding a day to the last month of the year, eleven times in the course of a thirty-year cycle. Within this there are eleven years of "abundance" with 355 days, occurring at years 2, 5, 7, 10, 13, 16, 18, 21, 24, 26, and 29. The other nineteen years in this thirty-year cycle remain of standard length.

صُورَةُ الخُسُوفِ الكُلِّى

تقدير الهيئة اذليه وقدرت باهرة لم يزليه تاريخ هجرت خورشيد اورنك اسمان بنوت وماه فلك مسير
برج رسالت عليه اطيبا البخيه خبرترنك بيك ايكيوز التبشى سنه هجرى يرسنه لى القعده سنك حب البقيه
اول دردنجى بازار رايرتسوكيجه سى غروبم بركر تشمدل بدى ساعت اون دقيقه انطباعنده قمر بوز برج جوزا ده عقده
زنده انخسافه ابتدا سكز ساعت يكروى بش دقيقه كذارنده بالكليه منخسف اولرق مكته اغان طقوز ساعت بش دقيقه
كذارنده وسط خسوف متحقق اولوب طقوز ساعت اللى دقيقه مرورنده انجلايم بيشلوب اون ساعت اللى طقوز دقيقه
ختامنه تماما منجلى اولرلرق روى قمرده خسف وكدر درتدندن اثر قالميه ذلك تقدير العزيز العليم

الاحكام

Ottoman imperial calendar drawn
in 1844 by Mehmet Sadullah
for Sultan Abdulmecid I.

50

الاختيار					الطوالع	الخمسة المتفرقة
مطالعة آيات رفع صدقات	جوزا	٤	٨	بثه	اخي برد الجوزا	شاهد عم دوام دعاء اولوب استلحت
تمتع وتجارت تتبع كتب وصنعت	ثور	٥	٩	بثه	حضيض مشتري	اجتماع البحر المرئيه اولد تأكنار ايله
سعد		٦	١٠	بثه	ميلاد النبي يلدر	جوابات اوكان بديدار الدين واستقبال
		٧	١١	بثه	تحويل شمس حمل	زياب الجمله في رطوبتد بهارده وحصولات
حضور واستراحت فراغ وعزلت		٨	١٢	بثه	ظهور دورالقمر	وبار رفو ودر باد شدت دخي واردهوهوا
حاجت از فريقات سبله شراي حيوان		٩	١٣	بثه		زمستان اولجغنه كاردنده ايام اولوب وبعضاننه
					والله اعلم الخ الدر	كي جواسان ايله

صورة الخسوف الكلي

مشيت الربية ربانيه وصنايع بديعه حكيمه ايله تاريخ هجرت نبويه عليه اكمل التحيه حترتلرنك بيك ايكيوز التمنجي سنه سنه اكرم ماه جمادى الاولسنك بالرؤيه اون بشنجي جمعه ارتسي كيجه سي غروبا قريب اوج ساعت قرق التي دقيقه مرور ذه تمه منزلذبرج قوسده عقده رأسده انخسانه اغاز دردت ساعت قرق طقوز دقيقه كذرانده بالكليه منخسف اولوب مكثه ابتدا ايده رك بش ساعت يكرمي بدي دقيقه كذرانده وسط خسوف مخققي اولوب التي ساعت بش دقيقه معبورنده انجلاء باشليوب يدي ساعت سكز دقيقه انطباقنده تماما مجلي اولوب في صفحه قمره ذلك خسوفدن اثر قاليه ذلك تقدير العزيز العلم

الاحكام

چون برج خسوف قوس وطالع وسط خسوف برج احوت خسوف مدبري اولوب قمر نه قتجره دن مشتري وشركي ثوابتل مخذ عنقا وقمر بعد الخسوف مركز نجم جسد رأس ايله مسعود اولدي دكا لابد رله تعالى اعلم بوخسوفك اثري كثرى يا فتوس وحوت برجلرينه منسوب بلا اقاليم ديار اوله كه عض اصفهان وارمنيه مصري وبلاد عجم وخراسان وكوفه وبغداد ومصر واسكندريه سمتلرنده اولوب اهاليلر مبيانده فساد وفتنه وحيل وخدعه ودهاوننده جدل ومناقشه واسكانده ارض مهنه وباديه نشينانده رنج ومنارعه وكبرا ورؤسا نده زحمت ومشقت واكا نسبه كثرت ايله اضطراب احوال الرنيه لكن افق استام اوز ره محسوب اولان طالع وسط خسوفنده مشتري تدبيرنك سعادتيله بوانفنده مضر ني قليل اولدر قا اسلامبول واطرافنده واقع محالك سكاننده امر بالمعروف ونهي عن المنكر رعايت ودعاي شرعيه ده دقت وقضاه وعلما ميانده دين ومذهبه متعلق مباحثاتنده كثرت وقوعنه بوخسوفك مدت تأثيري بلاد مذكوره لره اوج اي اوله اى برك اولوب معظم تأثيري خليهة خسوفدن اللى ايكي كون مرورنده واقع اوله والله تعالى اعلم

حقيقة الامور وهو عليم بذات الصدود

THE HEBREW CALENDAR

The chief characteristic of the lunisolar Hebrew calendar is its large number of dualities, leading to several duplicate timescales. The moon measures the months, and nomads naturally base their lives around its course; the sun, meanwhile, measures the years and determines the seasons, and settled populations organize their lives around its course. The Hebrew calendar harmonizes all these measurements. It was originally worked out on the basis of secret calculations known only to the Sanhedrin, the grand court and legislative assembly of Jerusalem. The priests would appoint two observers whose responsibility it was to track the moon and signal the precise moment when the smallest first sliver of the crescent moon appeared. The Sanhedrin than officially decreed the "neomenia", or first day of the lunar month, the *Molad*. This oral declaration was then transmitted by means of beacons lit from hilltop to hilltop.

This eminently imprecise process was plagued by inaccuracy, time differences, and interference from counter-beacons lit by enemies, among other distractions, all leading to considerable confusion. The subsequent diaspora of the tribes of Israel over a significantly larger geographical area further increased the obstacles, and the time duly came when accuracy became a fundamental imperative, to be applied by means of universal rules shared by all Jewish people everywhere.

Traditionally, history attributes the establishment of the Hebrew calendar to Rabbi Hillel II in 359 CE, or 4119 in the Jewish calendar. Before him, in 433 BCE, the Greek astronomer Meton of Athens had developed a calculation for merging the lunar and solar cycles, in which 6,490 days were divided into 235 lunar months representing 19 years of two types. To work out the type of any individual year, the date had to be divided by 19 in order to indicate whether it was a common or embolismic year (see the table on page 55). As his starting point, Hillel II picked at random a date for the creation of the world and designated it the *Anno Mundi* (AM), the rabbinic era of creation, also called the Jewish era. Inspired by the words of Genesis, based on the known or supposed chronology indicated by the Bible – the Torah counts the generations from Adam – this date was fixed at Monday, October 7, 3761 BCE. Set two days, five hours and 204 *halakim* (the *helek* or *chelek* (pl. *halakim* or *chalakim*) is the 3 1/3-second time unit that divides the hour into 1,080 parts and serves as the basis for calculating the Hebrew calendar) after this date, the first theoretical moon technically began the Hebrew calendar. The calendar is designed to encompass seven millennia: one for each of the six days of the creation of the world, and one for the seventh day, that of Shabbat. The year is celebrated twice: in spring, the season of germination and flowering, at the first pilgrimage feast, Pesach (Passover); and at the "head of the year", Rosh Hashanah, the start of the civil year, 1 Tishri, anniversary of the *Anno Mundi*.

Finally, Hillel also instated rules stating that Rosh Hashanah must never fall on a Sunday, a Saturday, or a Friday; Yom Kippur must never fall on a Friday or a Sunday; Pesach is always on the 15th of Nissan; and Rosh Hashanah always on the 1st of Tishri.

Nonetheless, ancient studies and rigorous recent research, backed up by a plethora of references and documentation (Sacha Stern, *Calendar and Community*, Oxford University Press,

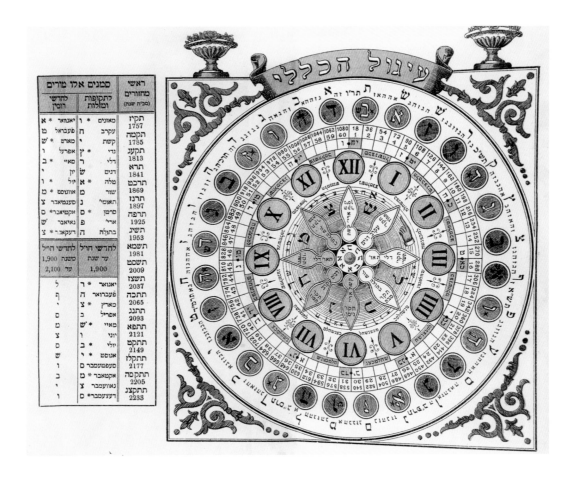

2001. Sylvie-Anne Goldberg, *Clepsydra, Essay on the Plurality of Time in Judaism*, Stanford University Press, Stanford CA, 2016, especially pp. 339–43.), pose strong challenges to the role of this legendary patriarch, whose existence is not documented by any verifiable historical source, and in particular the contemporary Palestinian and Babylonian versions of the Talmud. The fourth century CE yields a body of proof of considerable importance for the history of the Jewish calendar, including notably Christian sources relating to the establishment of the date of Easter – one of the key moments in the development of the Jewish calendar is also being the date when Christians decided

Above Astronomical table showing the movements of the planets. YIVO Institute for Jewish Research, New York.

to make Easter coincide with Pesach (Passover). It is impossible to pinpoint the existence of a single inventor of the fixed Hebrew calendar in one radical movement. The whole process was a gradual one: between late Antiquity and the early Middle Ages, the diaspora of the Jews was a gradual and widespread phenomenon, from Judea to Galilee, Babylon, Egypt, North Africa, and western Europe. During this founding period, the issues of cohesion and solidarity among the various rabbinic communities gained an extreme urgency. At the heart of these concerns, the calendar played a role of eminent importance in cementing the unity of a scattered people. The path towards a single Hebrew calendar was slow and gradual, involving numerous twists and turns and much scholarly controversy. Today, this unique calendar remains faithful to its unifying role, ensuring respect for the values of Jewish culture.

THE PERPETUAL HEBREW CALENDAR

Year 1 of the Hebrew calendar begins on October 7, 3761 BCE. This Monday is considered in Jewish tradition as the day when God created the world. It is calculated according to chronological and genealogical data, and details given in the Bible concerning the age of certain figures. The Jewish calendar is lunisolar. Its complexity lies in the combination between the 354-day lunar year and the solar year of 365 days, or 366 in leap years.

Centuries are spread over seven millennia. There are two types of Jewish year: common and embolismic. Within these two types, there are three distinctive qualities: defective or hollow, regular or normal, abundant or full. Some months are always full, others always hollow, and still others both full and hollow. Finally, the intercalation of Adar II – meaning the thirteenth 30-day month increasing the days of the year from 353 to 375 in a regular year – repeats the month of Adar according to the so-called Metonic cycle, comprising nineteen years divided into twelve common years and seven embolismic years. All types are linked invariably to a particular figure indicated in the recapitulative table. The type of year can be determined by dividing its number by nineteen: the year is common if the remainder is 1/2/4/5/7/9/10/12/13/15/16/18; the year is embolismic if the remainder is 0/3/6/8/11/14/17/19.

There are twelve or thirteen lunar months. The twenty-four-hour day begins with the appearance of the first star and ends the following twilight. The *helek* or *chelek,* plural *halakim* or *chalakim,* is the unit dividing the hour into 1,080 parts. This number is divisible by all numbers except 1 and 7. It also allows for the transposition of the lunar cycle into a whole number of units. The days of the week, in the Jewish faith, do not bear a name but instead a number. The week begins on on Sunday, day one, and ends with the start of the Shabbat, at sunset/twilight on Friday, day six, to twilight/sunset on Saturday, the only day that has a name: *Shabbat*, meaning literally cessation, or rest.

Various restrictions/additional constraints are involved in the establishment the Jewish calendar and must be respected. Rosh Hashanah – New Year, Tishri 1– must not fall on a Friday, nor a Saturday, nor a Sunday. The retrograde date of Yom Kippur, the Day of Atonement, must not fall on a Friday or a Sunday; in this case, the date is moved. The golden number indicates the position of the year within the Metonic cycle. The age of the Hebrew year: 5775 corresponds to 2014-2015 of the Gregorian calendar (Tishri 1= September 29th). The Molad is the exact moment when the first sliver of the crescent moon appears. It is indicated as the first line on the dial.

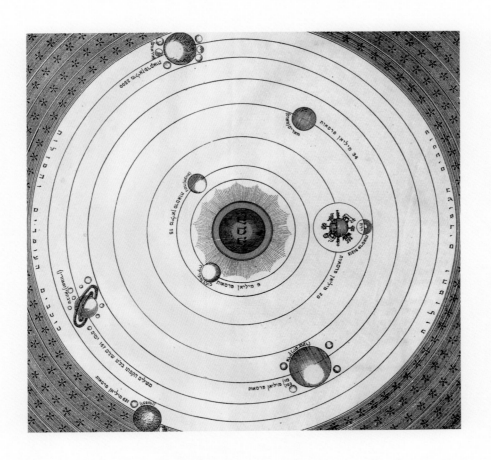

Diagrammatic representation of the Hebrew calendar
blue
the four invariable months with 30 days
red
the two variable months with 29 or 30 days
green
variation of adar and adar ii/ vé'adar or adar rihon & adar sheni
brown
the four invariable months with 29 days
purple
order of the months according to the lunisolar calendar: tishri 1
black
order of the months according to the solar calendar: nissan 1

GREGORIAN MONTH	JEWISH MONTH		COMMON YEAR 1/2/4/5/6/7/9/10/11/12/13			EMBOLISMIC YEAR 3/6/8/11/14/17/19		
			Defective	Regular	Abundant	Defective	Regular	Abundant
Sept / Oct	TISHRI	1/7	30	30	30	30	30	30
Oct / Nov	'HECHVAN	2/8	29	29	30	29	29	30
Nov / Dec	KISLEV	3/9	29	30	30	29	30	30
Dec / Jan	TEVET	4/10	29	29	29	29	29	29
Jan / Feb	CHEVAT	5/11	30	30	30	30	30	30
Feb / March	ADAR RISHON	6/12	29	29	29	30	30	30
Feb / March	ADAR SHENI	13/13	–	–	–	29	29	29
March / April	NISSAN	7/1	30	30	30	30	30	30
April / May	IYAR	8/2	29	29	29	29	29	29
May / June	SIVAN	9/3	30	30	30	30	30	30
June / Jul	TAMOUZ	10/4	29	29	29	29	29	29
Jul / Aug	AV	11/5	30	30	30	30	30	30
Aug / Sept	ELOUL	12/6	29	29	29	29	29	29
			COMMON YEAR 1/2/4/5/7/9/10/11/12/ 13/15/16 ou 18			EMBOLISMIC YEAR 0/3/6/8/11/14/17/19		
			Defective	Regular	Abundant	Defective	Regular	Abundant
	TOTAL OF DAYS		353	354	355	383	384	385

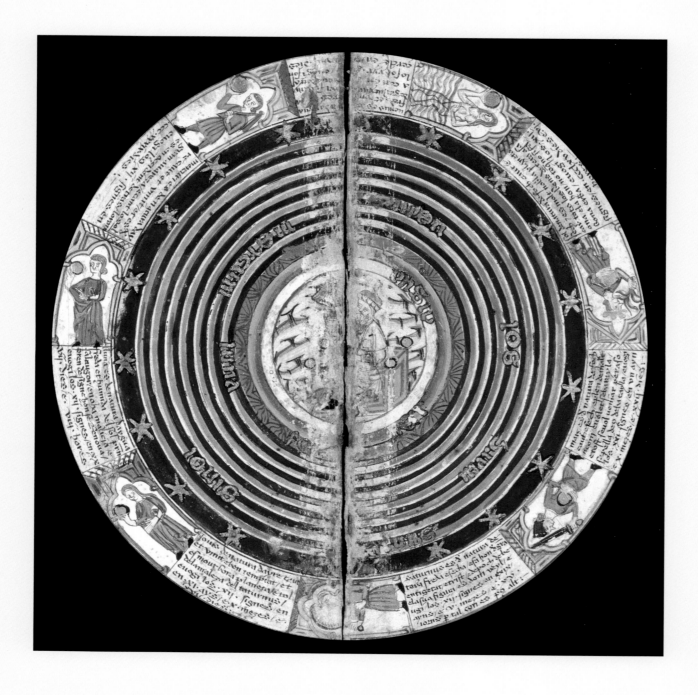

Above Geocentric representation of the universe, according to which the Earth is surrounded by the orbits of the seven planets (Moon, Mercury, Venus, Sun, Mars, Jupiter and Saturn) in the order adopted by Ptolemy. Abraham Cresques, astronomic calendar, *Catalan Atlas*, 1375.

Facing page, top The Hebrew week.

Facing page, center Table of the Metonic cycle as applied in the Caliber 3750. The perpetual calendar from 5774 to 5792, or 2014 to 2032, is recorded on 15 discs. After 19 years there is a time lag of 8 hours behind the lunar cycle and of 10 hours behind the solar cycle. After 16 Metonic cycles, the time lag is approximates one day.

Facing page, bottom Table of concordance between the Hebrew and Gregorian calendars for 19 years from the year 5774/2014. As the Jewish year begins in September, the Gregorian calendar straddles two years. The Gregorian calendar dates for Yom Kippur, as indicated by the Caliber 3750, are shown in red.

HEBREW DAY	NAME	SYMBOL-LETTER	GREGORIAN DAY
Day 1	Yom rishon יום ראשון	א	Sunday
Day 2	Yom shéni יום שני	ב	Monday
Day 3	Yom shlishi יום שלישי	ג	Tuesday
Day 4	Yom révi'i יום רביעי	ד	Wednesday
Day 5	Yom hhamishi יום חמישי	ה	Thursday
Day 6	Yom shishi יום שישי	ו	Friday
Day 7	Yom Shabbat יום שבת	ש	Saturday

YEARS	MONTHS WITH 30 DAYS	MONTHS WITH 29 DAYS	TOTAL NUMBER OF DAYS	NUMBER OF YEARS
2 defective common years	5	7	353	1/5
5 regular common years	6	6	354	18/2/10/13/16
5 abundant common years	7	5	355	4/7/9/12/15
3 defective embolismic years	6	7	383	8/14/17
1 regular embolismic year	7	6	384	6
3 abundant embolismic years	8	5	385	19/3/11

JEWISH YEAR	JEWISH DATE OF YOM KIPPUR (always from the evening of 9 Tishri to the evening of 10 Tishri)	GREGORIAN YEAR (from September)	GREGORIAN DATE OF YOM KIPPUR
5774		2013–2014	Friday October 3–Saturday October 4, 2014
5775		2014–2015	Tuesday Sept. 22–Wednesday September 23, 2015
5776		2015–2016	Tuesday October 11–Wednesday October 12, 2016
5777		2016–2017	Friday September 29–Saturday September 30, 2017
5778		2017–2018	Tuesday Sept. 18–Wednesday September 19, 2018
5779		2018–2019	Tuesday October 8–Wednesday October 9, 2019
5780		2019–2020	Sunday September 27–Monday September 28, 2020
5781		2020–2021	Wednesday Sept. 15–Thursday September 16, 2021
5782		2021–2022	Tuesday October 4–Wednesday October 5, 2022
5783		2022–2023	Sunday September 24–Monday September 25, 2023
5784		2023–2024	Friday October 11–Saturday October 12, 2024
5785		2024–2025	Friday October 1–Saturday October 2, 2025
5786		2025–2026	Sunday September 20–Monday September 21, 2026
5787		2026–2027	Sunday October 10–Monday October 11, 2027
5788		2027–2028	Friday September 29–Saturday September 30, 2028
5789		2028–2029	Tuesday Sept. 18–Wednesday September 19, 2029
5790		2029–2030	Sunday October 6–Monday October 7, 2030
5791		2030–2031	Friday September 26–Saturday September 27, 2031
5792		2031–2032	Tuesday Sept. 14–Wednesday September 15, 2032

THE GREGORIAN CALENDAR

The ancient Egyptian solar calendar lay at the origins of the Roman calendar, which preceded the calendar we now use. In making their calculations, the Egyptians made greater reference to the star Sirius than to the moon or the sun, as well as to the regular flooding of the Nile. They managed to establish a year of twelve months of thirty days each, to which they added five extra days (*epagomenae*) intercalated between the other days of the week, and which remained nameless. They soon found they were failing to keep up with the sun in its course and the rising waters, however. The Egyptians nonetheless established a chronology that was close to being reliable. The first Roman calendar dates back to the birth of Rome, in 753 BCE, under Romulus. The year was very short, with ten months, four of thirty days and six of thirty-one days, making a total of 304 days. After Romulus, Numa Pompilius (c.751–c.672 BCE) introduced a 365-day year, calculated by adding the month of January with twenty-nine days and February with twenty-eight, so making the start of the year closer to the winter solstice than to the spring equinox.

Numa Pompilius also established intercalations of forty-five days in four years, but these were applied in a pragmatic and opportunistic way, often coinciding with political interests, such as the reduction or extension of one jurisdiction or magistracy or another. The problems posed by the establishment of a calendar were not of any particular interest to the Romans, but on the other hand they could not do without one. The College of Pontiffs and some monarchs more than others applied themselves to the problem, which had become all too obvious: at one point there was a difference of as much as sixty-seven days between the start of the civil year and that of the solar year.

In 45 BCE Julius Caesar, a great reformer, made significant advances in the field by enlisting the services of the Greek astronomer Sogisenes of Alexandria. This calendar, known as the Julian calendar, boasted a number of advantages, including its perpetual nature, since it was as reliable for standard years as for leap years. Still based on the path of the sun, it set the official start of the year at January 1 and the number of days as 365 days and a quarter. Every four years, it doubled the sixth day – *sextili* – before the kalends of March, so introducing a month of February of twenty-nine days, and thereby creating the idea of the leap year that is still in place to this day. Yet it did not alter the rhythm of the months, the only change being to the names of two months at a later date, when Quintilis became Julius (July), in honour of Julius Caesar, and Sextilis became Augustus (August), in honour of Augustus. The irregular distribution of the days divided into kalends, ides and nones was retained. The kalends were the first day of the month; the nones the seventh day of March, May, July and October, and the fifth day of the other months; and the ides were the thirteenth day of March, May, July and October, and the fifteenth day of the other months. This irregular distribution made these days difficult to count – an effect that was to disappear under pressure from the Catholic Church. The week of seven days – *septimana* – as described in Genesis was imposed as the norm, and Sunday, the last day of the week, was declared the day of rest, whereas in the Hebrew calendar the last day of the week was the day of Shabbat.

Over fifteen hundred years were to pass without any major difficulties with the calendar. But the over-long Julian year maintained a disparity that grew steadily worse, to become a genuine incovenenience in the Middle Ages. The date of the Christian Easter, with its close links with the renewal of nature and the resurrection of Christ, was progressively slipping towards summer. Something needed to be done in order to fix the spring equinox at March 21, and to establish a rule to eliminate the ten-day lag behind the astronomical year. The Renaissance proved an auspicious time to embark on a reform that was to establish the long-term dominance of the Gregorian calendar. The Council of Trent, held under Pope Paul III in 1545, had already attempted to find a solution, but without success. This period of outstanding astronomers was at last to see the emergence of a pope who was determined to do what was necessary to settle once and for all the issue of the disparity between calculations that were inaccurate and the constant path of the sun. Like Julius Caesar, Pope Gregory XIII (Bologna 1502–Rome 1595) was a modernizer with a reforming spirit. Grasping the problem by the horns, he put in place all measures necessary for finding a solution. He set up a council of scholars, presided over by Cardinal Guglielmo Sirleto, one of the key figures of whom was the German Jesuit mathematician Christoph Klau (Bamberg 1536–Rome 1512), better known as Christopher Clavius. In 1603, Clavius published his work on calendar calculations in a treatise entitled *Calendarii Romani Gregoriani explicatio*.

It was decided that Thursday October 4, 1582 would be followed immediately by Friday October 15. Thus ten historic days simply disappeared. One of the main changes of the Gregorian calculations as compared with the Julian calendar was in the occurrence of leap years, the idea being to eliminate three days in four hundred years. The four-yearly rhythm was retained.

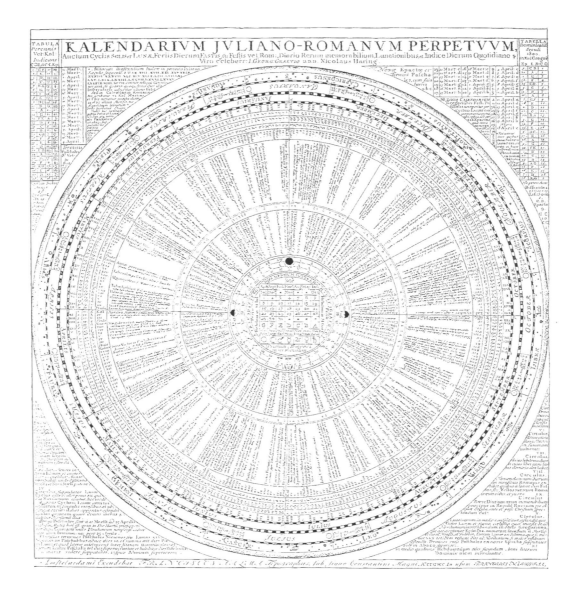

Only the first years of centuries that were divisible by four, such as 1600 and 2000, would be kept as leap years, while 1700, 1800 and 1900 became common years. The calculations currently cover a period of ten thousand years, which at the present pace means that there will still be three days to be eliminated. This will be achieved by making the years 4000, 8000 and 16000 common years rather than leap years.

The scholars assembled by Gregory were also concerned about the date of Easter. Adopted by Christianity from Judaism, Easter celebrates the resurrection of Christ that is the foundation of the Christian faith. While the reform finalized by Clavius set out to correct a disparity that was reduced to three days in ten thousand years, it above all enabled the pope to fix officially the distribution of the moveable religious feast days that were calculated from the date of Easter. Thanks to research conducted by Aloysius Lilius, also known as Luigi Lilio, a multi-talented Italian scientist from Calabria, Clavius was able to fix this complex date as the first Sunday after the full moon following the spring equinox, that is in the five-week period following March 21. If the full moon fell on a Sunday, Easter would come a week later.

Above Perpetual Julian calendar showing all past and future dates. Eighteenth-century engraving.

THE GREGORIAN WEEK

The seven-day period of the week stems from the twenty-eight-day lunar cycle divided by four. This rhythm is believed to have been adopted by Babylonians, whose example in this respect was followed by Jews, Christians and Muslims.

A process of standardization has been carried out more recently in order to facilitate time calculations and date exchanges between computer software programmes.

The first of the fifty-two weeks of the year is the one containing the first Thursday of that year. Contrary to the standardization of the number of weeks and order of days, the Reference 57260 watch features a week indication that displays the number of the week from one to 52 and that of the day of the week from one to seven, through separate mechanisms.

The number of the day is linked to its position in the sequence of days of the week. Taking for example the first week of the year 2013, January 1 was a Tuesday. Tuesday was therefore day one, Wednesday day two, etc. The display of the number of the day in the week on the Reference 57260 watch takes into account disparities of this nature.

DAY OF THE WEEK	ETYMOLOGY	NUMBER OF THE DAY
Monday	Lunae dies / day of the moon	DAY 1
Tuesday	Martis dies / day of Mars, day of Tiw (Norse god)	DAY 2
Wednesday	Mercuri dies / day of Mercury/day of Wodan (Germanic god)	DAY 3
Thursday	Jovis dies / day of Jupiter / day of Thor (Norse god)	DAY 4
Friday	Veneris dies / day of Venus, day of Frige (Anglo-Saxon goddess)	DAY 5
Saturday	Saturnis dies / day of Saturn / day of Shabbat	DAY 6
Sunday	Solis dies / day of the Sun	DAY 7
	Dominica dies / Lord's Day	

THE GRADUAL AND ALMOST UNIVERSAL ADOPTION OF THE GREGORIAN CALENDAR

This acceptance of the notion of a calendar that would be common to all, over and above religious beliefs and key events in the devotional calendars, was not a steady and untroubled process, but instead proved lengthy, laborious and random. It is an indication of just how sensitive issues relating to the imposition of a calendar can be, impinging as they do on the deepest beliefs of different cultures. The two reasons generally advanced to explain the adoption of the Gregorian calendar as the universal measure of time are on the one hand the growing dominance of the Western world in the scientific field; and on the other hand an economy that was able to regulate trade more easily between far distant lands. The Protestant and Orthodox churches were not to follow Gregory in this adventure, however (see below).

While the Gregorian calendar has played a powerful unifying role, as we have seen, it is nevertheless not perfect, and there have been various short-lived attempts to reform it. In 1793, the Republicans in France imposed a decimal system, giving the months and days poetic names inspired by nature, before gradually abandoning the attempt after thirteen years. In 1806, Napoleon reverted to the Gregorian calendar. In 1852, the French philosopher Auguste Comte suggested separating the calendar from any religious practices and making it strictly secular. He invented an even more imperfect system – based on the figure thirteen – that was adopted by nobody. In 1887, inspired by the work of Georges Armelin and Émile Manin, the French astronomer Camille Flammarion developed a universal calendar that was taken up

COUNTRY	YEAR
Italy and Portugal	1582
France and Lorraine	1582
Catholic state and cantons of Germany and Switzerland, Savoy, Belgium, Artois and Flanders	1582
Holland and Zeeland	1583
Prussia	1583
Austria	1584
Poland	1586
Hungary	1587
Scotland	1600
Catholic Swiss Valais	1655
Denmark and Norway	1700
Switzerland: Zurich, Bern, Basle, Geneva	

COUNTRY	YEAR
Great Britain, Ireland and eastern USA	1752
Sweden	1753
Albania	1872
Japan	1873
Korea	1895
Taiwan	1912
Bulgaria	1916
Western USSR	1917
Baltic States	1918
Yugoslavia	1919
Eastern USSR	1920
Greece	1923
Turkey	1927
China	1949

Chart showing the progressive adoption of the Gregorian calendar.

again in 1927 by the League of Nations. But this was a reform requiring too many profound changes in deeply ingrained customs: a fixed calendar of thirteen months of four weeks; and a universal calendar of four 91-day trimesters that nonetheless remained fairly close to the Gregorian calendar. Its distinctive contribution was the ritualizing of the first day of the month. December 31, the 365th day of the year, was called a "blank day" outside the normal calendar; in other words it was abolished. The day to be added every four years and corresponding to leap years was always June 31, while Easter was fixed on April 8.

Above *The committee for the reform of the calendar in 1582*, painted panel depicting Pope Gregory XIII enthroned, Archivio di Stato di Siena.

Today, the Gregorian calendar continues to co-exist alongside other calendars. The Jewish calendar is the official calendar of the State of Israel. The Islamic calendar is applied in parallel in various countries of Africa and the Middle East. In the major Asian countries, the distinctive calendars in India, China, Vietnam and Japan – which operates on the basis of imperial eras – also govern religious life. Very few countries do not currently use the Gregorian calendar. Among them are Ethiopia and Eritrea, Afghanistan, Iran, Pakistan and Saudi Arabia.

REFERENCE 57260

Reference 57260 is a masterpiece of unimaginable complication and technical innovation, one that looks at least as far into the future as it looks back into the past for inspiration.

It is a celebration of human ingenuity, technical mastery, and, yes, life itself, with its beating mechanical heart. Conceived, developed, manufactured, prototyped, finished, and assembled over a breathtaking period of eight years by a team of three of Vacheron Constantin's master watchmakers, this all-encompassing study of the past, present, and future of horology is stamped with the prestigious Hallmark of Geneva.

The symbolic name of Reference 57260 comprises two numbers: 57 for the number of complications and functions it features, and 260 for Vacheron Constantin's anniversary year in 2015. The technical innovations included in Reference 57260, some of which have never been seen before in a mechanical timepiece, resulted in more than 10 patents being filed.

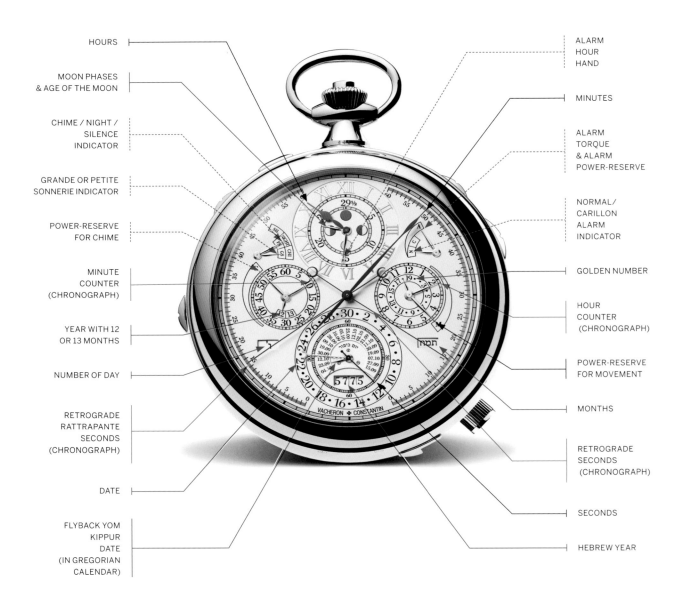

CHAPTER 3 — *Reference 57260*

HOURS

MOON PHASES
& AGE OF THE MOON

CHIME / NIGHT /
SILENCE
INDICATOR

GRANDE OR PETITE
SONNERIE INDICATOR

POWER-RESERVE
FOR CHIME

MINUTE
COUNTER
(CHRONOGRAPH)

YEAR WITH 12
OR 13 MONTHS

NUMBER OF DAY

RETROGRADE
RATTRAPANTE
SECONDS
(CHRONOGRAPH)

DATE

FLYBACK YOM
KIPPUR
DATE
(IN GREGORIAN
CALENDAR)

ALARM
HOUR
HAND

MINUTES

ALARM
TORQUE
& ALARM
POWER-RESERVE

NORMAL/
CARILLON
ALARM
INDICATOR

GOLDEN NUMBER

HOUR
COUNTER
(CHRONOGRAPH)

POWER-RESERVE
FOR MOVEMENT

MONTHS

RETROGRADE
SECONDS
(CHRONOGRAPH)

SECONDS

HEBREW YEAR

——————— HEBRAIC PERPETUAL CALENDAR
- - - - - - - - - STRIKING-WORK
——————— CHRONOGRAPH

RETROGRADE DATE
(PERPETUAL
CALENDAR)

DAY /
NIGHT
(2ND TIME ZONE)

24 TIME ZONES
(WORLD TIME)

HOURS AND
MINUTES
(2ND TIME ZONE)

DAYS (PERPETUAL
CALENDAR)

SUNRISE
INDICATION
(FOR THE CITY OF
THE OWNER)

LENGTH OF DAY
(FOR THE CITY OF
THE OWNER)

EQUATION OF TIME

ARMILLARY SPHERE
TOURBILLON

CELESTIAL SKY CHART
RETROGRADE DATE AND
SIDEREAL INDICATIONS

IN RED, THE LAST
DAY OF EACH
MONTH

LEAP
YEAR

NUMBER OF THE DAY
OF THE WEEK

MONTHS (PERPETUAL
CALENDAR)

52-WEEK INDICATOR

PERPETUAL MONTHS
& DAYS,
ZODIAC SIGNS,
SEASONS,
EQUINOXES &
SOLSTICES

LENGTH OF NIGHT
(FOR THE CITY OF
THE OWNER)

SUNSET
INDICATION
(FOR THE CITY
OF THE OWNER)

REFERENCE 57260

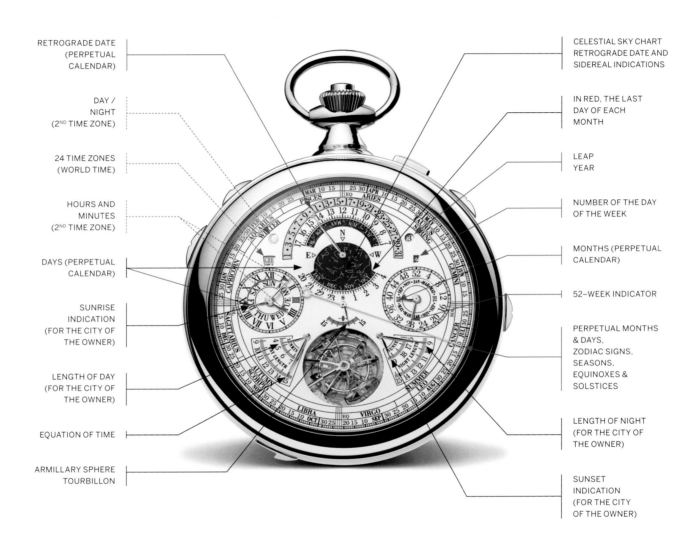

—————————— PERPETUAL CALENDAR
------------------------ WORLD TIME

69

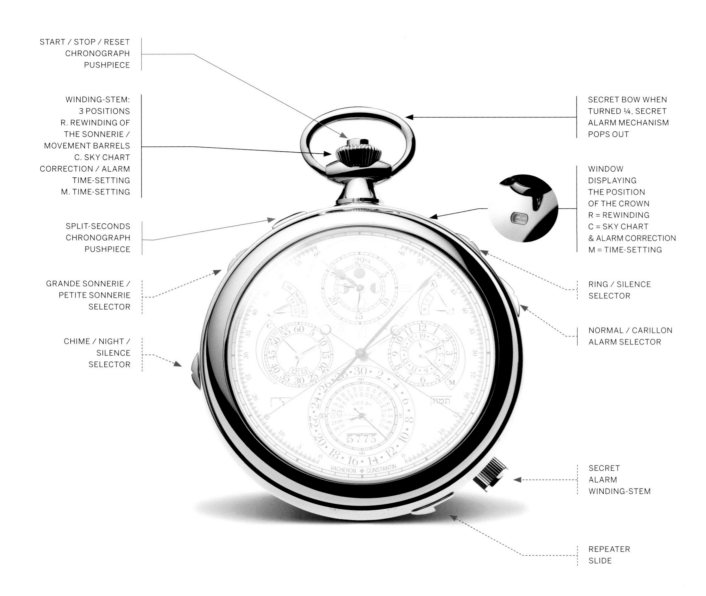

START / STOP / RESET
CHRONOGRAPH
PUSHPIECE

WINDING-STEM:
3 POSITIONS
R. REWINDING OF
THE SONNERIE /
MOVEMENT BARRELS
C. SKY CHART
CORRECTION / ALARM
TIME-SETTING
M. TIME-SETTING

SPLIT-SECONDS
CHRONOGRAPH
PUSHPIECE

GRANDE SONNERIE /
PETITE SONNERIE
SELECTOR

CHIME / NIGHT /
SILENCE
SELECTOR

SECRET BOW WHEN
TURNED ¼, SECRET
ALARM MECHANISM
POPS OUT

WINDOW
DISPLAYING
THE POSITION
OF THE CROWN
R = REWINDING
C = SKY CHART
& ALARM CORRECTION
M = TIME-SETTING

RING / SILENCE
SELECTOR

NORMAL / CARILLON
ALARM SELECTOR

SECRET
ALARM
WINDING-STEM

REPEATER
SLIDE

————————— HEBRAIC PERPETUAL CALENDAR
- - - - - - - - - - STRIKING-WORK
————————— CHRONOGRAPH

SELECTION OF FUNCTIONS AND SETTINGS
ON THE PRINCIPAL DIAL

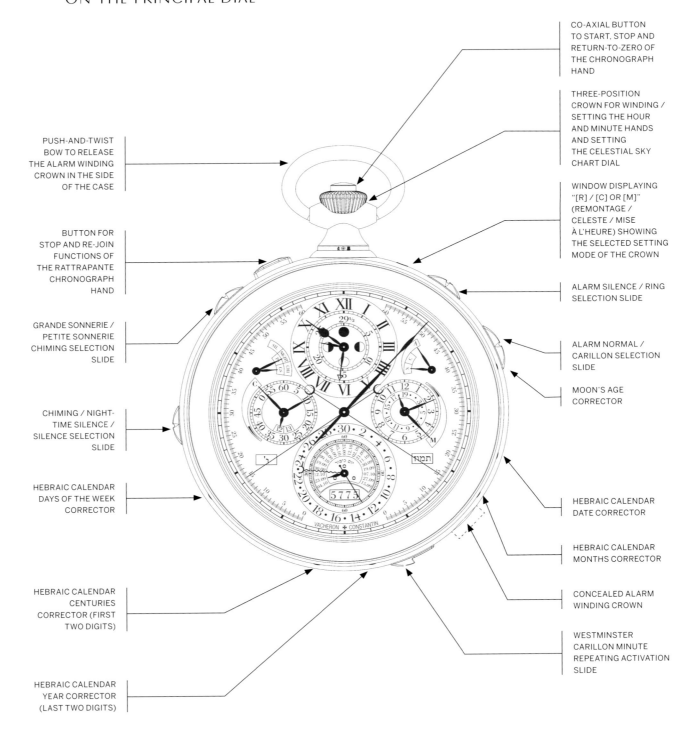

CO-AXIAL BUTTON
TO START, STOP AND
RETURN-TO-ZERO OF
THE CHRONOGRAPH
HAND

THREE-POSITION
CROWN FOR WINDING /
SETTING THE HOUR
AND MINUTE HANDS
AND SETTING
THE CELESTIAL SKY
CHART DIAL

PUSH-AND-TWIST
BOW TO RELEASE
THE ALARM WINDING
CROWN IN THE SIDE
OF THE CASE

WINDOW DISPLAYING
"[R] / [C] OR [M]"
(REMONTAGE /
CELESTE / MISE
À L'HEURE) SHOWING
THE SELECTED SETTING
MODE OF THE CROWN

BUTTON FOR
STOP AND RE-JOIN
FUNCTIONS OF
THE RATTRAPANTE
CHRONOGRAPH
HAND

ALARM SILENCE / RING
SELECTION SLIDE

GRANDE SONNERIE /
PETITE SONNERIE
CHIMING SELECTION
SLIDE

ALARM NORMAL /
CARILLON SELECTION
SLIDE

MOON'S AGE
CORRECTOR

CHIMING / NIGHT-
TIME SILENCE /
SILENCE SELECTION
SLIDE

HEBRAIC CALENDAR
DAYS OF THE WEEK
CORRECTOR

HEBRAIC CALENDAR
DATE CORRECTOR

HEBRAIC CALENDAR
MONTHS CORRECTOR

HEBRAIC CALENDAR
CENTURIES
CORRECTOR (FIRST
TWO DIGITS)

CONCEALED ALARM
WINDING CROWN

WESTMINSTER
CARILLON MINUTE
REPEATING ACTIVATION
SLIDE

HEBRAIC CALENDAR
YEAR CORRECTOR
(LAST TWO DIGITS)

HEBRAIC CALENDAR
CENTURIES
CORRECTOR (FIRST
TWO DIGITS)

HEBRAIC CALENDAR
DAYS OF THE WEEK
CORRECTOR

GREGORIAN
PERPETUAL
CALENDAR
RETROGRADE
DATE AND MONTHS
CORRECTOR
SIMULTANEOUSLY
CORRECTING THE
EQUATION OF
TIME, SEASONS,
SUNRISE / SUNSET
AND DAY AND NIGHT
INDICATIONS

HEBRAIC CALENDAR
DAYS OF THE WEEK
CORRECTOR

HEBRAIC CALENDAR
DATE CORRECTOR

HEBRAIC
CALENDAR MONTHS
CORRECTOR

WORLD-TIME DUAL
SIMULTANEOUS
HOURS FROM
GMT AND CITY
CORRECTOR

DAYS OF THE WEEK
CORRECTOR

WESTMINSTER
CARILLON MINUTE
REPEATING
ACTIVATION SLIDE

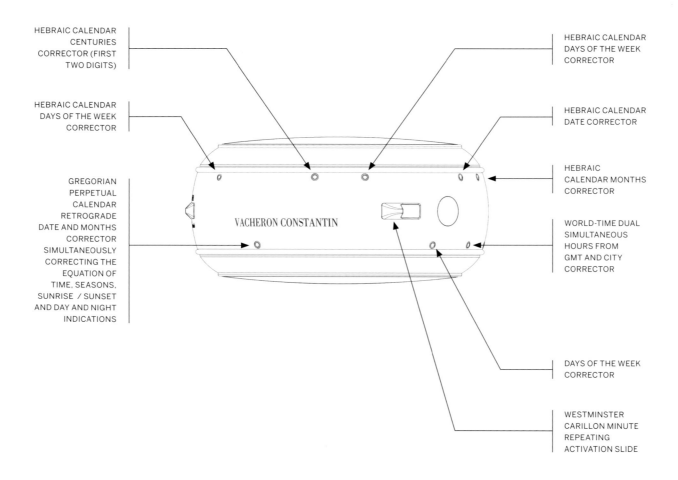

VACHERON CONSTANTIN

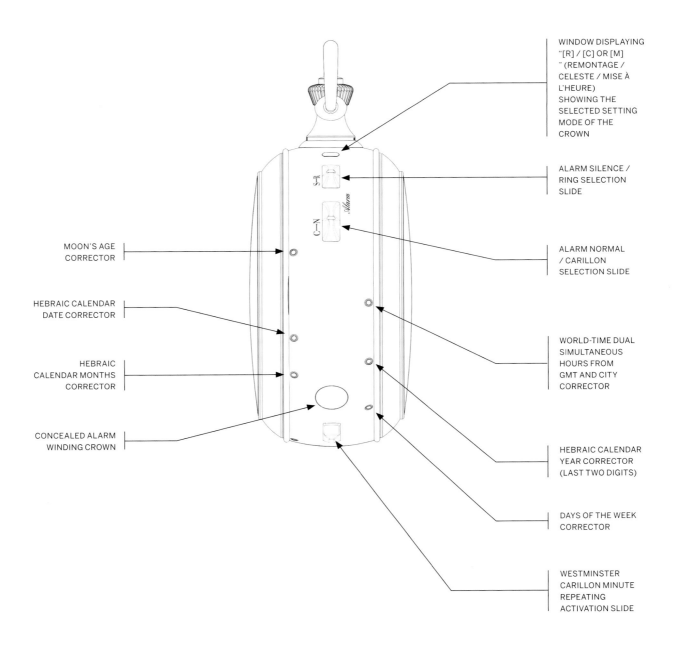

WINDOW DISPLAYING "[R] / [C] OR [M] " (REMONTAGE / CELESTE / MISE À L'HEURE) SHOWING THE SELECTED SETTING MODE OF THE CROWN

ALARM SILENCE / RING SELECTION SLIDE

ALARM NORMAL / CARILLON SELECTION SLIDE

MOON'S AGE CORRECTOR

HEBRAIC CALENDAR DATE CORRECTOR

HEBRAIC CALENDAR MONTHS CORRECTOR

CONCEALED ALARM WINDING CROWN

WORLD-TIME DUAL SIMULTANEOUS HOURS FROM GMT AND CITY CORRECTOR

HEBRAIC CALENDAR YEAR CORRECTOR (LAST TWO DIGITS)

DAYS OF THE WEEK CORRECTOR

WESTMINSTER CARILLON MINUTE REPEATING ACTIVATION SLIDE

REFERENCE 572260

GREGORIAN PERPETUAL CALENDAR / ISO CALENDAR NUMBER OF THE DAYS OF THE WEEK CORRECTOR

GREGORIAN PERPETUAL CALENDAR / ISO CALENDAR NUMBER OF THE WEEK CORRECTOR

GREGORIAN PERPETUAL CALENDAR RETROGRADE DATE AND MONTHS CORRECTOR SIMULTANEOUSLY CORRECTING THE EQUATION OF TIME, SEASONS, SUNRISE / SUNSET AND DAY AND NIGHT INDICATIONS

BUTTON FOR STOP AND RE-JOIN FUNCTIONS OF THE RATTRAPANTE CHRONOGRAPH HAND

GRANDE SONNERIE / PETITE SONNERIE CHIMING SELECTION SLIDE

CHIMING / NIGHT-TIME SILENCE / SILENCE SELECTION SLIDE

HEBRAIC CALENDAR DAYS OF THE WEEK CORRECTOR

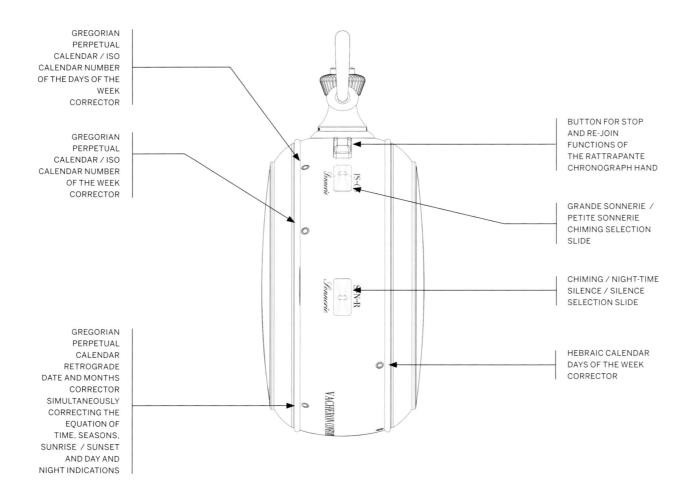

TIME

1	Regulator-type hours, minutes and seconds for solar mean time
2	Visible spherical armillary tourbillon regulator with spherical balance spring
3	Armillary sphere tourbillon
4	12-hour second time zone hours and minutes
5	Indication for 24 world cities for world time
6	Day and night indication for the 12-hour world time

PERPETUAL CALENDAR

7	Gregorian perpetual calendar
8	Gregorian days of the week
9	Gregorian months
10	Gregorian retrograde date
11	Leap-year indication and four-year cycle
12	Number of the day of the week (ISO 8601 calendar)
13	Indication for the number of the week within the year (ISO 8601 calendar)

HEBRAIC PERPETUAL CALENDAR

14	Hebraic perpetual calendar with 16 x 19-year cycle
15	Hebrew number of the day
16	Hebrew name of the month
17	Hebrew date indication
18	Hebrew secular calendar
19	Hebrew century, decade, and year
20	Indication for the number of months in the Hebraic calendar year (12 or 13 months)
21	Indication for the Golden Number within the 19-year Metonic cycle
22	Indication for the date of Yom Kippur in the Gregorian calendar

ASTRONOMICAL CALENDAR

23	Indications for the seasons, equinoxes, solstices and signs of the zodiac with "sun" hand
24	Sky chart (calibrated for the city of the owner)
25	Sidereal time hours
26	Sidereal time minutes
27	Hours of sunrise (calibrated for the city of the owner)
28	Hours of sunset (calibrated for the city of the owner)
29	Equation of time
30	Length of the day (calibrated for the city of the owner)
31	Length of the night (calibrated for the city of the owner)
32	Phases and age of the moon, one correction every 1027 years

RATTRAPANTE CHRONOGRAPH

33   Retrograde fifths of a second chronograph
(1 column wheel)

34   Retrograde fifths of a second rattrapante
chronograph (1 column wheel)

35   2-hour counter (1 column wheel)

36   60-minute counter

ALARM

37   Progressive alarm with single gong
and hammer striking

38   Alarm strike / silence indicator

39   Choice of normal alarm or carillon
striking alarm indicator

40   Alarm mechanism coupled to the carillon
striking mechanism

41   Alarm striking with choice of grande
or petite sonnerie

42   Alarm power-reserve indication

WESTMINSTER CARILLON

43   Carillon Westminster chiming with
5 gongs and 5 hammers

44   Grande sonnerie passing strike

45   Petite sonnerie passing strike

46   Minute repeating

47   Night silence feature (between 22.00 and 08.00
hours – hours chosen by the owner)

48   System to disengage the striking barrel
when fully wound

49   Indication for grande or petite sonnerie modes

50   Indication for silence / striking / night modes

ADDITIONAL FEATURES

51   Power-reserve indication for the going train

52   Power-reserve indication for the striking train

53   Winding crown position indicator

54   Locking mechanism for the striking train

55   Winding system for the double barrels

56   Hand-setting system with two positions
and two directions

57   Concealed flush-fit winding crown
for the alarm mechanism

REFERENCE 57260

One of the most ingenious – and some might say greatest – man-made objects in the world, Reference 57260 was created using the principles of traditional watchmaking alongside resolutely twenty-first-century concepts. Within the 57 functions and complicated elements, we find multiple calendars, including a Hebrew calendar the like of which has never been seen in a mechanical timepiece; a double retrograde split-seconds chronograph, also a new and unique development; and modified, reinterpreted, and redesigned existing complications such as the armillary tri-axial tourbillon. What we we do not find are any off-the-rack standards – not even the exquisitely finished tourbillon cage, which is shaped like Vacheron Constantin's Maltese cross emblem – or the "simple" indication of hours, minutes, and seconds, which is interestingly displayed regulator-style on Reference 57260.

Pages 78–79 Mechanical manual-winding Caliber 3750, entirely developed and produced by Vacheron Constantin, comprises more than 2,800 parts and 242 jewels and its plates: Plate 150: Chronograph Plate 250: Perpetual Gregorian calendar Plate 350: Chronograph & Perpetual Hebrew calendar Plate 550: Astronomical calendar

The realization of Reference 57260 also required an enormous and exceptional understanding of both mathematics and craftsmanship. As it sets a new benchmark in horology, this was a given. However, without the encounter that takes place between an important collector capable of commissioning such a work of art and the expertise of a great Maison comprising experienced artists, this would never have been possible.

Vacheron Constantin's history has been filled with extraordinary, complicated, and elegant timepieces, all of which take their places of honour in the lineage of the world's oldest continuously operating watch Manufacture – though none of these quite compares to Reference 57260, a record-setting watch if there ever was one. The pages that follow offer a relatively comprehensive explanation of the most interesting and innovative complications that this timepiece offers.

While complications may often be best avoided in life, in the context of a timepiece that reaches – and perhaps even exceeds – the pinnacle of the art of watchmaking, being the most complicated specimen in the world is a prestigious description.

Reference 57260 displays 57 complications and functions on two solid silver dials. The pure timekeeping functions are displayed on the front dial using traditional blued steel hands. For easier reading, the hours, minutes and seconds are configured in "regulator" style so that they can be read off separately. The regulator dial layout derives from the dials of the precision clocks invented in the late eighteenth century; these were used in observatories and scientific laboratories to provide accurate and clear time readings.

Facing page The hours, minutes and seconds are shown in separate regulator-type display mode, inspired by the precision clocks invented in the late eighteenth century.

The golden Roman numerals marking the hours are located in a chapter ring at 12 o'clock; the minutes, displayed by the thicker of the central sweep hands, are displayed with the help of the railway track scale around the outermost perimeter of the dial. Railway track seconds are displayed in a subdial at 6 o'clock, driven from the tourbillon escapement positioned directly underneath it.

Pages 82–83, facing page and above
The Reference 57260 watch comprises 57 complications and functions displayed on two sides. The front shows the Hebraic perpetual calendar, the chiming complications as well as the split-seconds chronograph functions. The hours are indicated by gold Roman numerals on a subdial at 12 o'clock, the minutes by the broadest central hand on a railway track scale around the rim of the dial, and the seconds driven by the tourbillon escapement, on the railway track scale of the 6 o'clock subdial.

Pages 86–87, facing page and above
On the back, the Reference 57260 watch gives pride of place to the triple-axis tourbillon with spherical balance spring at 6 o'clock. The double calendar invented by Vacheron Constantin combines two distinct functions that can be read off simultaneously: the traditional perpetual Gregorian calendar with

12 months, 52 weeks and 7 days, and the ISO 8601 professional calendar. The hours and minutes around the world are displayed in 12-hour mode so as to ensure perfect legibility, complemented by day/night and selected city indications appearing through two separate apertures.

The regulator, comprising the balance and escapement of a watch movement, is the sub-assembly that controls the precision of a timepiece. The Reference 57260 regulator ensures the highest degree of precision available to the science of horology today, thanks to its elegant triple-axis tourbillon with spherical balance spring. Happily, the fascinating motion of the constantly revolving tourbillon is also completely visible through the cutaway at 6 o'clock on the back dial.

The overall "spherical" appearance of the tourbillon is characterized by its special balance spring, whose properties contribute to stabilizing its accuracy. Vacheron Constantin named this spherically shaped tourbillon "armillary" in tribute to Antide Janvier, since it bears a visual similarity to the interlocking circles and rings of the scientific instrument known as the armillary sphere, an instrument for which the eighteenth-century French watchmaker was particularly known. Despite its serious and logical shape, this tourbillon still contains one of Vacheron Constantin's most playful elements: a tourbillon cage in the shape of the Maltese cross, the company's emblem. Crafted in ultra-light aluminum, once every fifteen seconds the tourbillon revolves so that the Maltese cross becomes fully visible through the dial opening.

The tourbillon was originally patented by Abraham-Louis Breguet in 1801 specifically to improve the timekeeping accuracy of pocket watches, which were usually kept in a vertical position in the wearer's pocket and therefore most relentlessly subjected to the effects of gravity. The timekeeping ability of a watch can be affected by changes in its position as the normal effect of gravity pulls down on the balance, creating very small distortions that, in turn, affect accuracy of timekeeping; this effect is known to watchmakers as positional error. The tourbillon is essentially a compensatory revolving platform making a full rotation in one minute upon which the whole escapement is mounted; in the triple-axis tourbillon, as the name suggests, the escapement is rotated in three planes at once. Its purpose is to completely eliminate the effects of gravity on the balance and escapement. Gravitational errors are already quite successfully equalized in the standard single-axis tourbillon, as it turns the balance on its own axis in all possible vertical positions during the course of each 60-second rotation. In the three-axis tourbillon, positional errors caused by gravity are completely negated, because the balance wheel, hairspring, and escapement constantly rotate, and are never fixed in any one position. The effect of gravitational pull is therefore regularized and equal; the watch can thus be regulated to keep time totally unaffected by random change in position during use.

While Breguet famously invented the concept, some German watchmakers improved upon it, including Alfred Helwig (1886-1974), technical director of the Deutsche Uhrmacherschule (German School of Watchmaking) in Glashütte, who experimented with the tourbillon mechanism in attempts to improve its functionality. In 1920, Helwig invented what is now commonly known as the flying tourbillon, which comprises a free-standing cage supported from only one side, without a bridge. This invention made it possible to create a much thinner movement, while also allowing the observer to view the mechanism at work. However, it was Helwig's pupil Walter Prendel, one of only four students to graduate from the Deutsche Uhrmacherschule in Glashütte with honours, who in 1928 first constructed a tourbillon with the cage slightly tilted out of the vertical. This

Facing page The "armillary" spherical tourbillon is a tribute to the eighteenth-century French watchmaker Antide Janvier. The watchmakers at Vacheron Constantin have created the most supremely elegant mechanism that displays a three-dimensional constantly rotating sphere moving with the utmost delicacy simultaneously in three directions. Appropriately, the watchmakers have also chosen to use a spherical balance spring which not only adds to the elegance of the mechanism, but also – thanks to its distinctive properties – contributes to the accuracy of the watch.

meant it was never in a completely vertical or horizontal position, thereby eliminating the two most extreme positional error variations. Prendel's invention led to significant improvements in rate.

But the concept of a tourbillon rotating on more than one axis was first expressed in 1921 by Sir David Salomons, the legendary collector and authority on Breguet, who wrote, "Breguet invented the tourbillon, which gets rid of certain positional errors, but if the balance again turned a complete revolution out of its plane at the same time as the tourbillon was work-ing, then all positional errors disappear…" Not being a watchmaker, Salomons could never put his idea into practice himself. But it was this idea that must have inspired British watchmaker Anthony Randall more than fifty years later, in 1978, to construct his first dual-axis tourbillon; he obtained a patent for it in 1982. Based on Randall's work, another British watchmaker, Richard Good, made the first triple-axis tourbillon. Both Randall's dual and Good's triple-axis tourbillons were large-scale and fitted into carriage clocks, meaning they did not have to endure sudden changes in position like wristwatches. Their research forms the foundation for all of today's work with multiple-axis tourbillons, the most engaging of visual creations. Furthermore, the expiry of the patents for those first multiple-axis tourbillions has allowed modern-day watchmakers to further develop the triple-axis tourbillon, which has now culminated in the extraordinarily sophisticated armillary three-axis tourbillon incorporated in Vacheron Constantin's historical masterpiece.

Facing page Caliber 3750, entirely designed and developed within the Manufacture, is graced with finishing that reflects the finest traditions of Haute Horlogerie. All of the 2,800 or so components are meticulously hand-finished, including those invisible to the naked eye.

Two further inventions with historic horological heritage have been included in the Refer-ence 57260 escapement: a spherical hairspring and the use of diamonds for the jewels of the pallets in the escapement. The spherical hairspring used in the armillary tourbillon echoes and enhances the overall spheroid design of the tourbillon, but it also has a practical purpose. It was invented in 1814 by Swiss watchmaker Jacques-Frédéric Houriet, who thereby demonstrated that a spherically shaped hairspring provides the closest thing possible to perfect isochronism. The aim of the watch-maker is to make a watch "isochronous," a term implying that the watch's timekeeping is unaffected by amplitude fluctuations or the oscillating balance's swing, caused when the watch goes from a fully wound state to that of unwind. When the mainspring is fully wound, the balance swings at its widest arc; as the mainspring's power subsides, the amplitude naturally decreases. Adjustment for isochronism involves making the hairspring in such a way that the balance's swings consistently take the same amount of time to travel to and fro, independent of amplitude. As Houriet showed, the spherically formed hairspring is most effective in making a watch isochronous; however, the spherical hairspring is very difficult to manufacture and as a result is only ever found in the most sophisticated watches.

The pallet fork of this watch's escapement is fitted with diamond pallets, which are low-friction and very hard-wearing, as well as adding value and an appreciable rarity factor. Because diamond, the hardest substance known to man, is exceedingly difficult and costly to cut into the precise and specific shape needed to make the pallets, only a few watches have ever been made with diamond pallets. This component boasts a historical context both in the wider history of watchmaking and in that of Vacheron Constantin. The properties of diamond for use as escape-ment pallets were first recognized by the legendary English watchmaker John Harrison (1693–1776) in the mid-eighteenth century. Harrison's H4, which eventually claimed the Longitude Prize, was fitted with diamond pallets. But this was not the inspiration for Reference 57260; here, Vacheron Constantin's watchmakers were inspired by the Chronomètre Royal, a wristwatch the company made in small numbers in the mid-twentieth century. The movements of those watches were also fitted with diamond pallets.

PERPETUAL CALENDAR

The Reference 57260 perpetual calendar displays the date (via a retrograde hand at 6 o'clock on the back dial), the day of the week, the month, and the current position within the four-year leap-year cycle of the Gregorian calendar. The latter is displayed in a small window on the dial showing a number between 1 and 4, which indicates the current year within the four-year cycle (4 representing the leap year).

Unlike a normal watch calendar, which must be corrected by the wearer at the end of any month with fewer than 31 days, this mechanism "perpetually" self-corrects the length of each month without manual intervention: 30 days for April, June, September, and November and 31 days for January, March, May, July, August, October, and December. The tricky month of February is also automatically corrected for either its usual 28 or the leap year's 29 days.

ISO 8601 BUSINESS CALENDAR

In addition to the Gregorian perpetual calendar, Reference 57260 is fitted with a newly invented Vacheron Constantin calendar mechanism: the business calendar system known as ISO 8601. This is the first time that the ISO 8601 calendar's week and day displays have been crafted as a function within a timepiece.

The ISO 8601 business calendar is a specific system set by the International Organization for Standardization, for use mainly in international business and financial sectors. The purpose of this standard is to provide an obvious method of representing dates to avoid misinterpretation between countries with different conventions for writing numeric dates and times.

In the ISO 8601 business calendar, the number of the week within the year and the number of the day within the week replace the traditional calendar month and date. On the Reference 57260 dial, the week number is found on the outside track of the subdial at 3 o'clock on the back dial, while the number representing the day of the week is indicated by a number between 1 (Monday) and 7 (Sunday) in the square aperture directly above it.

Facing page The perpetual calendar date is indicated by a retrograde hand sweeping over the sky chart and returning to its starting point at the end of each month.

An ISO year usually comprises 52 weeks, but it can also have 53 full weeks when New Year's Day falls on a Thursday (Wednesday or Thursday in leap years), which occurs every five or six years. In the ISO calendar, week 1 always contains the first Thursday of the year as well as January 4. The last week of the ISO calendar contains the last Thursday and December 28. This system requires the user to adopt a different mode of interpretation: for example, if the regular calendar displays Thursday, September 17, the ISO calendar will show day 4 in the aperture and week 38. The ISO format for this date is 2015-W38-4.

THE NUMBER OF THE WEEK AND THE DAY, PROVIDING TWO CALENDAR OPTIONS WITH THE CHOICE OF EITHER GREGORIAN OR ISO 8601 BUSINESS CALENDAR

As a significant first for the world of watchmaking, Vacheron Constantin has invented a dual calendar mechanism with two separately functioning yet mechanically integral options that can be read at the same time – the traditional Gregorian perpetual calendar with 12 months, 52 weeks and 7 days, alongside the business calendar system known as ISO 8601.

This is the first time that the ISO 8601 calendar has been made as a watch function. Its creation and incorporation as one half of the dual calendar system has required not only extremely complex calculations, but also the practical skills of the Vacheron Constantin watchmakers in designing and translating their theory into a working and easily readable function.

The Gregorian perpetual calendar, which automatically corrects itself for the appropriate number of days in the month and the leap years, employs a retrograde date display, days of the week and months dials and a leap year window displaying a number between 1 and 4 in the leap year cycle.

The ISO 8601 business calendar is a specific system founded by the International Organization for Standardization, for use mainly in the international financial sector – for example in company accounting for tax years, payment of wages or rents due on a weekly basis, the planning of projects in weekly cycles, and so forth. The purpose of this standard is to provide an unambiguous method of representing dates and times in order to avoid any misinterpretation of numeric representations of dates and times, particularly when data is transferred between countries with different conventions for writing numeric dates and times. When times are also required under the ISO system, they are given using the 24-hour system and with time-zone information where necessary.

When the ISO 8601 mode is employed, the number of the week within the year and the number of the day within the week take precedence over the traditional calendar month and traditional date. The number of the week is read from the dial concentric to the month indication, and the number of the day within the week is indicated by a number between 1 (for Monday) and 7 (for Sunday) in a window directly above the week dial.

The ISO system has a full cycle of 400 years, and employs a seven-day cycle with weeks starting on a Monday. However, an ISO year may have either 52 full weeks, or 53 full weeks when New Year's Day falls on a Thursday (Wednesday or Thursday in leap years), which occurs every five or six years. In the ISO calendar, week 1 contains the first Thursday of the year and always contains January 4. The last week of the year in the ISO calendar contains the last Thursday and always includes December 28. This system requires the user to adopt a different way of interpreting the information given; if the calendar displays Thursday, September 17, for example, the ISO calendar will read as day 4 in the aperture (because Thursday is the fourth day) and week 38 on the week dial.

Facing page In the ISO 8601 mode, the number of the week within the year and the number of the day within the week take priority over the month and date in the traditional calendar. The number of the week is displayed on an outer dial, concentric with the inner dial indicating the months; the number of the day – from 1 (Monday) to 7 (Sunday) – is shown in an aperture just above the week dial.

THE NEW 12-HOUR AND MINUTE WORLD-TIME SYSTEM WITH DAY AND NIGHT INDICATION FOR 24 CITIES

In 1932 – although it is a little-known fact in the history of watchmaking – Vacheron Constantin became the first of the great watchmaking houses to produce a true world-time watch, using Louis Cottier's now familiar world-time mechanism with 24-hour indication, the system used almost exclusively ever since by all the foremost watch manufacturers. Continuing its tradition of harnessing the matchless minds and skills of their unparalleled team of watchmakers, Vacheron Constantin now introduces a wholly new and totally different system of world-time display, using a 12-hour indication designed and created entirely in-house in the Vacheron Constantin atelier. This new mechanism and display is compact and easy to read at a glance, eliminating the customary necessity for the entire watch dial to be devoted to the world-time function, and therefore allowing the possibility of combining it with any number of other complications. As with all true innovations, the simplicity of its design and ease of its use belie the ingenuity of the idea, which represents the first true alternative and improvement upon the world-time watch since the 1930s.

The adoption of Greenwich Mean Time in 1893 divided the globe into 24 time zones centered on London. Created initially as an aid to maritime navigation and then to the railways, with the advent of long-distance air travel and the worldwide telephone service this system became ever more relevant. In the 21ˢᵗ-century age of round-the-clock communication and international travel, a watch with world-time function has never been so useful.

As one of the functions of this important new Vacheron Constantin watch, the 12-hour second time zone dial is a smaller dial, separate from the main timekeeping dial, featuring only the Roman numerals I–12 instead of the full 24-hour day and night numerals as on most other world-time watches. Instead, a separate indicator window shows the user whether it is day or night in the chosen city. Another aperture window neatly replaces the usual ring-type city display of the Cottier system. Displayed in the aperture is a choice of 24 cities, each with its three-letter abbreviation along with its respective time deviation, plus or minus, from Greenwich Mean Time.

Facing page The 12-hour second time zone dial with separate day/night indicator window located in the 10 o'clock position is a first in watchmaking: the second time zone is used in conjunction with the digitally displayed world-time function which gives a choice of 24 cities and countries and their respective time deviations from Greenwich Mean Time. This extremely discreet 12-hour world-time system is the first invention of this kind since Louis Cottier's well-known 24-hour system invented in about 1935, and is therefore of major significance.

HEBRAIC
PERPETUAL CALENDAR

The Hebraic calendar works on the principle of the nineteen-year Metonic cycle, a period that almost exactly represents a common multiple of the solar year and lunar month. In a subdial at 6 o'clock on the Reference 57260 front dial, the Metonic cycle is displayed as a sector engraved with the sacred date of Yom Kippur – the holiest day of the Jewish calendar – for each of the nineteen years. The retrograde Yom Kippur hand returns to its starting position at the end of each nineteen-year period, at which time the engraved sector must be manually exchanged for the next from a series of nineteen additional sectors made for and included with the watch. Thus, the first sector plate comes back into use after nineteen cycles; the cycle continues this way in perpetuity.

To maintain the twelve-month lunar year's pace even with the solar year, a thirteenth leap (intercalary) month is added seven times during the nineteen-year cycle. Reference 57260 not only allows for the addition, but also shows the user whether the current one is a twelve- or thirteen-month year, via a hand and a "12/13" display situated within the chronograph minute subdial at 9 o'clock on the front dial.

In the Hebrew calendar, the months are based on lunar months of alternating lengths of either 29 (Marcheshvan) or 30 (Kislev) days. The perpetual date display with corresponding golden hand forms the outside ring of the Metonic sector subdial at 6 o'clock. The two apertures to either side of this subdial display the names of the days (left) and the months (right) in Hebrew.

A four-digit aperture within this subdial displays the Hebrew year, which is calculated from 3760 BCE (the first year of the Hebrew calendar – *anno mundi* – based on the Jewish year of creation). To calculate the present year in the Hebrew calendar, add 3760 to the Gregorian calendar year: 3760 + 2015 = 5775.

The innermost ring of the chronograph's hour totalizer subdial at 3 o'clock on the front dial displays what is known as the golden number in the Hebrew calendar, the number assigned to each year in the Metonic cycle's sequence. This function simultaneously indicates the leap years fixed within the nineteen-year cycle, shown by the numerals in which they occur: 3, 5, 7, 9, 11, 13, 15, 17 and 19. The other years are marked by dots.

Influenced by the ancient Babylonians, the Metonic cycle was calculated by the Greek astronomer Meton of Athens around 432 BCE. Within a period of nineteen years there are 235 lunar months equalling 6,940 days, making the two almost exactly a common multiple. The difference between nineteen solar years and 235 lunar months is only about two hours; therefore, the comparatively accurate Metonic cycle's error is only one full day every 219 years. Meton's calculations of the cycle were significant: by allowing a reliable calculation of the lunisolar calendar, it provides knowledge of when the thirteenth intercalary month should be inserted to keep the lunar year in pace with the solar year, thus maintaining the seasons at the same calendar times each year. Meton realized that the thirteenth month had to be added on seven occasions. Forming the basis of the Greek and Hebrew calendars, the cycle can also be used to predict eclipses and calculate the date of Easter.

Facing page The reliability of the lunisolar calendar is based on adding a 13th month (Adar 1), called an intercalary month, seven times during the 19-year cycle in order to keep the lunar year in step with the solar year and to maintain the seasons in the same periods each year. Ingeniously, the watch not only allows for this addition but also shows the user whether the current year comprises 12 months (common years) or 13 months (embolismic years) via an indicator hand and 12/13 display concentric with the chronograph minute register and counter hand in the 9 o'clock position.

Facing page The Hebraic perpetual calendar works on the principle of the 19-year Metonic cycle because 19 years is almost exactly a multiple of the solar year and lunar month over that period. The Metonic cycle (also called Golden Number) is displayed on the engraved sector at 3 o'clock.

Above The sacred date of Yom Kippur indicated in the Gregorian calendar each year, is represented by the corresponding retrograde hand at 6 o'clock, which returns to its starting point every 19 years, at which time the engraved sector is replaced by the next one. In the Hebraic calendar, there are fixed lunar months of 29 or 30 days alternately. Those of Cheshvan and Kislev can have 29 or 30 days, depending on the year. Here, the self-correcting date hand is concentric to the Yom Kippur sector and constant seconds. On either side of the date, two windows

indicate the number of days and months in Hebrew. The secular Hebraic calendar, which is displayed in a four-digit window below the Yom Kippur sector, is calculated from the supposed date of the creation of the world in 3760 BCE. Here, to calculate the year the watch was introduced according to the Hebraic calendar, 2015 was added to 3760, giving the year 5775. The Jewish New Year occurred in September 2015 and marked the start of the year 5776. Tishri is the first month of the Hebrew calendar.

105

HIGH-PRECISION AGE AND PHASES OF THE MOON

The Reference 57260 phases of the moon system requires correction only once every 1,027 years, when it has deviated by one full day. The four moon images within the subdial at 12 o'clock on the front dial display the lunar cycle, which is complete in exactly 29.5305882 days: new moon, first quarter, third quarter, and full moon. The surrounding ring displays the number of each elapsed day of the 29.5-day cycle, thus showing the moon's age.

The new moon occurs when the moon is positioned between the earth and sun; the three bodies are approximately aligned so the illuminated part of the moon is not visible from earth. At full moon, the earth, moon, and sun are in approximate alignment – just as with the new moon – but the moon is on the opposite side of the earth, so the sunlit part of the moon is facing our blue planet. The first- and third-quarter half moons occur when the moon is at a 90-degree angle to the earth and the sun, when exactly half of the moon is illuminated and half in shadow.

Below Within the center of the hour chapter-ring are four representations of the moon phases and also a hand indicating the age of the moon within its 29.5305882 day cycle. The Vacheron Constantin moon phase system requires correction only once every 1,027 years.

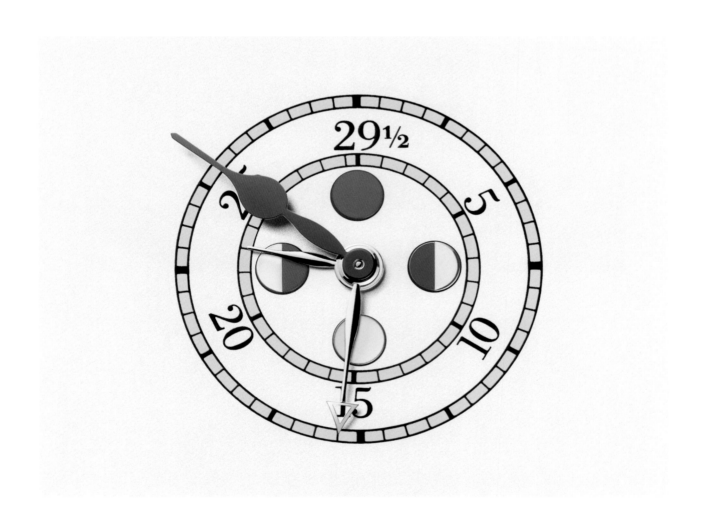

CELESTIAL SKY CHART
AND SIDEREAL TIME

The Reference 57260 celestial chart displays the precise constellations visible in the night sky from the geographical location of its owner's home. The months are inscribed in two 160° arcs above and below the sky chart; a red marking indicates the last day of each month.

The rotation of the star chart is governed by sidereal (star) time, which can be read using the corresponding 24-hour scale surrounding it. Choose a star at the appropriate time and track that same star as it rotates; the point where the chosen star is found in relation to the 24-hour scale indicates the current sidereal time. From a chosen observation point, a star in the night sky will always be found in the same position at the same sidereal time on any given night.

Sidereal time was traditionally used by astronomers and navigators; the sidereal day comprises the interval between two consecutive upper transits of the vernal point in the plane of the meridian. Since in practice this can be measured as the earth's rotation in relation to celestial objects, it is called sidereal or star time (*sider* means "star" in Latin). The sidereal day, measured in mean time, is 23 hours, 56 minutes, and 41 seconds long: thus the sidereal year contains one more day than the solar year.

Using the stars as a point of reference, sidereal time offers a more regular scale of time than that originating in using the sun as a reference. Naturally, the sidereal sky chart is mainly used during hours of darkness when constellations are visible; the main indications on Reference 57260 are therefore for the hours between 8:00 pm and 4:00 am.

Above The blue star chart in the upper half of the dial represents the night sky and the star constellations visible from the user's home city, with the months appearing around the edge. Sidereal time can be read off on a 24-hour outer scale.

SEASONAL ASTRONOMICAL INDICATIONS

This ingenious and precise multiple seasonal calendar and astronomic scale around the perimeter of one of the two main dials has three distinct indications that are read simultaneously, using the central gold hand identifiable by its sun counterpoise. The outermost scale is for the perpetual months of the year and their respective self-correcting number of days.

Concentric with this is the scale for the year, divided into periods of the Zodiac and additionally indicating the dates of the vernal (spring) and autumnal (fall) equinoxes, when day and night are approximately of equal length, and the summer and winter solstices, when the sun is at its highest or lowest point in relation to the celestial equator. The four seasons, spring, summer, autumn and winter, are indicated on a further inner concentric ring.

The two annual equinoxes occur in March and September each year. The March equinox, called the spring or vernal equinox in the northern hemisphere, falls on March 19, 20 or 21. The September, or autumnal, equinox falls on September 22, 23 or 24. The earth's axis is always tilted at an angle of approximately 23.5 degrees to the ecliptic, the imaginary plane created by the earth's path around the sun. On any other day of the year, either the southern hemisphere or the northern hemisphere tilts a little towards the sun. But on the two equinoxes, the tilt of the earth's axis is perpendicular to the sun's rays, and so day and night are nearly equal in length – hence the term "equinox".

The solstices and equinoxes are directly connected with the seasons. In many cultures, the solstices mark either the beginning or the midpoint of winter and summer. In the northern hemisphere, the summer solstice, around June 20/21, marks the day when the sun is highest in the sky and the longest day of the year; conversely at the winter solstice, around December 21/22, the sun is at its lowest point and the day is the shortest of the year.

Above and facing page Around the edge of the dial are three astronomic scales which are read using the central gold hand identified by its sun counterpoise. The outermost scale is for the months of the year and their respective number of days, while a concentric scale for the year divided into Zodiac sign periods additionally indicates the dates of the vernal and autumnal equinoxes and the summer and winter solstices. The inter-related four seasons are displayed on a further inner concentric ring.

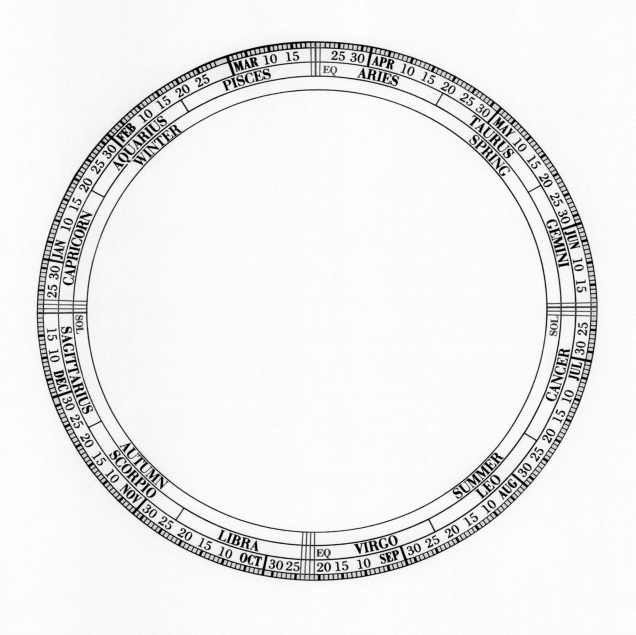

EQUATION OF TIME

The equation of time scale is visible just below the celestial sky chart, while the times of sunrise and sunset as well as the lengths of the current night and day are indicated in scales below this, to the left and right of the tourbillon cutaway. All these indications are likewise calibrated to the geographical location of the owner of the Reference 57260.

The equation of time, indicated by a small gold hand and a scale immediately above the tourbillon cutaway on the back dial, is formed by the discrepancy between apparent solar time and standard mean time (the even divisions of a clock or watch). Expressed in minutes, this discrepancy fluctuates during the course of a year, with mean time as much as 16 minutes and 33 seconds ahead (around November 3) and 14 minutes and 6 seconds behind (around February 12) solar time. Solar and mean time are equal on just four occasions each year.

Facing page The sector above the tourbillon aperture indicates the equation of time, showing the discrepancy between true solar time and standard mean time, which fluctuates during the year but can be ahead by as much as 16 minutes (around November 3) and behind by 14 minutes (around February 12). Solar and mean time are equal on just four occasions each year.

The hand's movement on the dial is governed by an irregularly shaped cam, which is driven from the mechanism for sidereal time. The equation of time displayed also corresponds to the season shown on the scale around the perimeter of the dial, indicated by a long gold hand decorated with a sun symbol; it, too, is driven by the sidereal time mechanism. Historically, knowledge of the equation of time was necessary for navigators, who observed the sun's altitude at a time noted according to a (mean time) clock or watch set in the sailor's home port.

The equation of time's discrepancy is caused by two elements: firstly, the equator's plane is inclined toward the earth's orbital plane; and secondly, the orbit of the earth around the sun is elliptical and not circular.

EQUATION OF TIME OWING TO OBLIQUITY

or the Earth's Tilt

If the earth's rotational axis were not tilted with respect to its orbit around the sun, the apparent motion of the sun along the ecliptic would fall directly on the equator, covering the same angles along the equator in equal time. This is not the case, however, since the angular movement is not linear in terms of time, because it changes as the sun moves above and below the equator. The projection of the sun's motion on to the equator will be at a maximum when its motion along the ecliptic is parallel to the equator at the summer and winter solstices, and will be at a minimum at the equinoxes.

EQUATION OF TIME OWING
TO UNEQUAL MOTION

or the Earth's Elliptical Orbit

The orbit of the earth around the sun is elliptical. The distance between the earth and the sun is at its minimum around December 31 and its greatest around July 1. The sun's apparent longitude changes most rapidly when the earth is closest to the sun. The sun will appear on the meridian at noon on these two dates, and so the equation of time owing to unequal motion will then be zero. The mean solar day, calculated by averaging all the days of the year, was invented by astronomers for convenience, so that the solar day would always be twenty-four hours. True solar time and mean solar time coincide four times a year, on April 16, June 14, September 1, and December 25. On these days, the equation will equal zero. On the remaining 361 days, the equation of time indicator must be used to indicate the difference between the two times. This positive and negative value is offset in the time of local noon, sunrise and sunset. Equation of time, often represented by a figure eight or "analemma", can be approximated by the following formula:

E = 9.87 * sin (2B) − 7.53 * cos (B) − 1.5 * sin (B), where B = 360 * (N-81) / 365, where N = day number, January 1 = day 1.

The times of sunrise and sunset and the lengths of the current night and day are driven by the same cam as that which calculates the equation of time.

111

DUAL SECTORS FOR SUNRISE, SUNSET, AND LENGTH OF DAY AND NIGHT

Few watches have the inbuilt capability to inform the owner of the times of sunrise and sunset and the length of the day and night in their home city throughout the year. For this very special watch, two dual sectors have been provided specifically for this purpose, driven by the perpetual calendar mechanism.

The mechanism automatically corrects the indications over the course of the entire year to show the correct time of sunrise and sunset and the length of day and night in each successive 24-hour period. Each sector has two corresponding gold hands operating from the same axis. The sunrise sector and hand for this watch indicate the changing time of sunrise throughout the year, from 4 am at its earliest until just before 8 am at its latest. Sunset is registered in the other sector, calibrated from 4 pm until around 7.30 pm, again depending on the time of year. The lower sectors are the indications for length of day and night, displaying the appropriate number of hours in the day from sunrise, and the number of hours in the night from sunset. If sunrise is at 4.30 am and sunset at 7.30 pm, for instance, the day length is 15 hours. From sunset at 7.30 pm to sunrise at 4.30 am the length of the night is 9 hours, with night and day therefore adding up to a precise 24-hour period.

Indications of the time of sunset and sunrise are governed by cam-based mechanisms geared to the perpetual calendar system, and are automatically corrected at midnight. The cams can be made to accommodate sunrise and sunset at any spot in the world chosen by the owner, and are bespoke-made during construction of the watch. The times indicated are within five minutes of true sunset or sunrise, which is when the sun's upper limb rests on the true horizon of an observer at sea level. True sunset or sunrise is normally corrected to allow for the refraction of the earth's atmosphere.

This fascinating mechanism, taken in the context of this spectacular watch, is relevant to another exceptional and unique complication to be revealed at the final unveiling of the complete watch.

Facing page and pages 114–15 Flanking the tourbillon aperture are two dual sectors for the time of sunrise and day length and time of sunset and night length in the user's home city. These indications are in fact another relevant factor in the Gregorian calendar, in which the days are calculated from the hours of light and darkness and not strictly set times.

CARILLON GRANDE
AND PETITE SONNERIE
WITH WESTMINSTER CHIME

Westminster chiming is the most complicated striking mechanism for the watchmaker to construct, requiring a sequence of five perfectly tuned steel gongs to transmit the sound, each gong being struck with a separate hammer regulated so that the carillon chiming is in complete harmony.

WESTMINSTER CHIMING AND MINUTE-REPEATING – The chiming mechanism strikes automatically at every passing quarter-hour, in the same manner as a full-size clock. With five hammers striking on the five finely tuned steel gongs, the sequence is the same as that of Big Ben, the world-famous clock of the Houses of Parliament in London (hence the name Westminster chimes). This watch follows the traditional Westminster chiming sequence and has two options to choose from:

GRANDE SONNERIE, in which both the hours and the quarter-hours are struck at every passing quarter-hour. At 9.45, for example, the full three-bar Westminster tune is struck (one bar of the tune for each elapsed quarter-hour), followed by nine single strikes for the elapsed hours.

PETITE SONNERIE, in which the hours are struck at the hour only, and quarter-strikes only on the quarter-hours. At 9.45, for example, the watch strikes the full three-bars of the Westminster tune, but no further strikes are sounded for the hours until the next full hour is reached.

A silence option can also be activated when no striking is required.

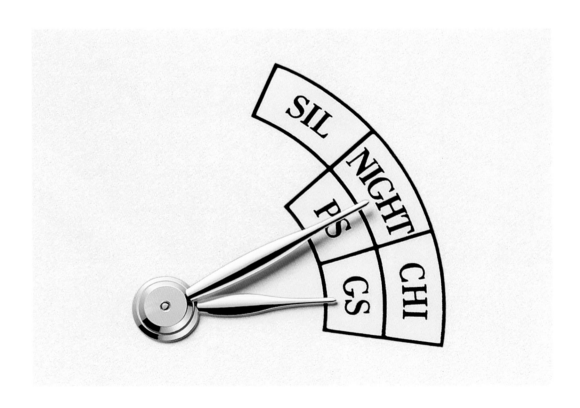

WESTMINSTER CARILLON MINUTE-REPEATING – The slide on the side of the case can be operated to activate the chiming whenever the user desires, a feature known in watchmaking as "repeating" because the current time is "repeated" by the striking mechanism. In this minute-repeating watch, the repeating sounds the time in the following order: quarter-hours, minutes and hours. At 9.48, for example, the minute-repeating will strike the full three bars of the Westminster tune because three quarter-hour periods have elapsed since 9 o'clock, followed by three further strikes for the three elapsed minutes since the last quarter-hour, and finally nine strikes for the elapsed hours.

NIGHT-TIME SILENCE FEATURE – The chiming mechanism incorporates a unique and very user-friendly new feature developed especially for this watch: the automatically activated "Night-Time Silence". This innovative system, unique to Vacheron Constantin, automatically engages so that between (say) 10 pm and 8 am it does not chime in order not to disturb its owner. The night-time silence function is the first to be automatically activated, without the need to manually set the chime or silence option. The precise hours of night silence are bespoke-set in-house at Vacheron Constantin before delivery of the watch.

Facing page and above Three striking modes are available. 1/ Striking – the watch chimes automatically at each passing quarter hour. With five hammers striking five finely tuned steel gongs, the chiming sequence is that of "Big Ben", the clock of the Palace of Westminster in London. 2/ Night silence – chiming automatically disabled from 10 pm to 8 am. 3/ Silence – chiming switched off when it is not desired. The owner can also choose between grande sonnerie (GS) and petite sonnerie (PS).

117

ALARM SYSTEM WITH CHOICE
OF CARILLON WESTMINSTER CHIME
OR SINGLE-STRIKE ALARM
OF DIFFERENT TONE

The Vacheron Constantin alarm system offers a sumptuous choice between a Westminster carillon or a conventional alarm. The carillon option provides a choice of either grande sonnerie or petite sonnerie. The normal alarm sounds on a single gong, which is an extra gong and not one of the five used for the Westminster chime. It is tuned at a different pitch to distinguish it from the Westminster gongs; likewise, an additional hammer sounds the single alarm strike.

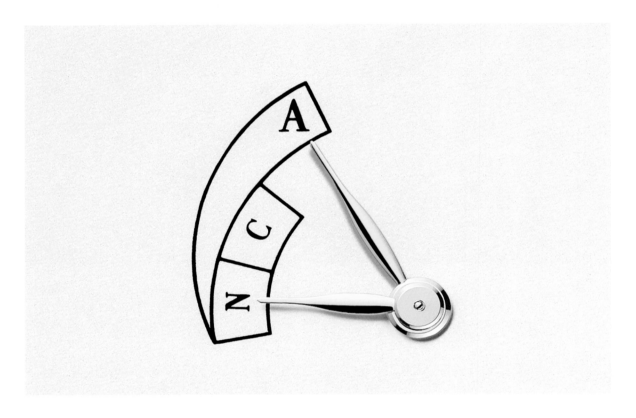

To wind the alarm mechanism, a never-before-seen element was set into the side of the case: a hidden winding button. As it is entirely flush-fitting, it does not disturb the line of the case, making an elegant solution. To wind the alarm, the button is released by depressing the bow above the crown and twisting it in a clockwise quarter turn; the button then pops out to protrude from the case at the 5 o'clock position, ready for use. The progress of the winding can be observed by the position of the alarm's power reserve hand; the button is pushed back in after winding. The ability to choose between a Westminster carillon and a single alarm strike is a feature unique to Reference 57260. When the alarm is triggered, it continues ringing until all the power from the alarm barrel is used.

Above and facing page In addition to the chiming mechanism, this model houses an integrally connected alarm system with separate power-reserve indication. The main feature of this Vacheron Constantin mechanism is that it allows a choice between either a traditional alarm on an additional differently tuned single gong with single hammer, or Westminster carillon full chiming alarm in either grande or petite sonnerie mode.

The alarm time is shown by a gold hand in the hour subdial of the main time display, while the alarm torque and power reserve is displayed on a scale at 2 o'clock on the front dial marked by an "A". This scale also shows whether the owner has chosen the normal alarm (N) or the carillon (C) function.

DOUBLE RETROGRADE
SPLIT-SECONDS CHRONOGRAPH

Reference 57260 is the first watch to be made incorporating Vacheron Constantin's double retrograde rattrapante chronograph, which is used in exactly the same way as a split-seconds chronograph – but includes a twist. While both hands work in unison and from the same axis, unlike all other split-seconds chronographs the two hands never actually meet but operate on two separate scales on opposing sides of the dial. In this respect, the chronograph can perhaps be best described as a "detached" split-seconds chronograph.

Operating the Chronograph – The chronograph can be used to time a single event or two events that begin simultaneously but do not necessarily end together. The unique feature of this chronograph is that although it functions like a split-seconds chronograph, the two hands never re-join in the usual way, instead each pointing to a separate scale.

Two arched retrograde chronograph scales, each numbered 0–60 and calibrated to show intervals of one-fifth of a second, are located along the left and right edges of the dial just inside the minutes railway track. Pressing the button in the crown starts both hands. Upon reaching the 60-second marks at the top of the scales, the hands instantaneously fly back to zero in typical retrograde manner. The Reference 57260 movement automatically compensates for the fractional time lapse created by the retrograde flyback action.

This retrograde chronograph function using two second hands is equivalent to the split-seconds function in all other rattrapante watches, even if it is completely different in both its design and operation. The hands travel across the scales in unison and symmetrically. The hand on the left side is stopped and started by pressing a button at 11 o'clock on the side of the case. If this button is pressed while the chronograph is running, the rattrapante chronograph hand stops and the timing can be read; this hand can be stopped independently of the primary chronograph hand at any required point to read an intermediate timing. On its release, the hand instantaneously jumps in a "catch-up" action to once again position itself symmetrically to the primary chronograph hand – just like a conventional pair of split-seconds chronograph hands. This action can be repeated as often as necessary throughout the timing period.

Twelve-hour (3 o'clock position) and sixty-minute (9 o'clock position) totalizer subdials record the elapsed minutes and hours when the chronograph is in constant operation, so that any event up to twelve hours in duration can be accurately timed to one-fifth of a second. When the button in the crown is pressed a second time, both hands stop. To reset both hands, the button in the crown is depressed a third time.

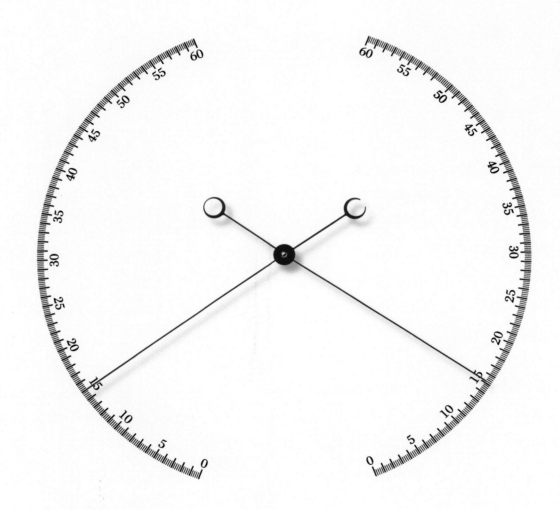

Faire mieux si possible.
Ce qui est toujours possible.

François Constantin
5 Juillet 1819

TECHNICAL DATA

REFERENCE	57260/000G-B046 Hallmark of Geneva certified timepiece
CALIBER	3750 Developed and manufactured by Vacheron Constantin Mechanical, manual-winding 72 mm (31'''½) diameter, 36 mm thick Approximately 60 hours of power reserve 2.5 Hz (18,000 vibrations/hour) More than 2,800 components 242 jewels
CALIBER PLATES	Plate 150: Chronograph Plate 250: Gregorian perpetual calendar Plate 350: Chronograph & Hebraic perpetual calendar Plate 550: Astronomic calendar
INDICATIONS	Time functions (6) Perpetual calendar functions: Gregorian and Hebraic (15) Astronomic calendar functions (9) Lunar calendar function (1) Religious calendar function (1) Chronograph (3 column-wheels) functions (4) Alarm functions (6) Westminster Carillon striking functions (8) Further functions (7)
CASE	18K white gold 98 mm diameter, 50.55 mm thick
DIAL	Metal Silvered opaline
NUMBER OF HANDS	Front: 19 / back: 12
ACCESSORIES	Delivered with a corrector pen and a magnifying glass
ADDITIONAL INFORMATION	Unique piece crafted on demand Total weight: 960 g

THE HALLMARK OF GENEVA

Representing far more than merely a certificate of origin, the Hallmark of Geneva is a guarantee of quality and excellence, established in 1886 and issued by an independent official body.

The Hallmark of Geneva recognizes high-quality watches developed and assembled in the canton of Geneva according to extremely stringent criteria relating both to the movement components and to the performance of the watch.

A four-fold consumer guarantee of origin, precision, durability and watchmaking expertise, the Hallmark of Geneva sets extremely high production standards serving to achieve the finest possible results in terms of reliability and aesthetics.

Since 1901, Vacheron Constantin has remained the most loyal representative of the prestigious Hallmark of Geneva.

POINÇON DE GENÈVE

À TOC WATCH

A dumb repeater watch in which a hammer strikes the inside of the case to produce a muffled sound. Invented by Julien Le Roy c. 1750.

ALARM

A pocket watch, wristwatch or clock that sounds automatically at a pre-set time. The alarm function regained popularity with the launch, by Eterna in 1908, of a wristwatch with an alarm.

ALL-OR-NOTHING PIECE

A system that prevents an insufficiently wound striking mechanism from striking too few hours.

AMPLITUDE

The distance between the two extreme points of a movement or periodic phenomenon.

ANNUAL CALENDAR WATCH

A full or partial simple calendar that automatically takes into account months with fewer than 31 days or leap years, but not leap years. It must be adjusted once a year.

ANTI-MAGNETIC

Describes a watch that is protected against magnetic fields.

APERTURE

A small opening in the dial.
In an aperture watch, various indications such as the month, moon phase, day, date, hour, minute, etc. are visible through these openings.

APPLIED CHAPTER (APPLIQUE)

Hour numerals or decorations that are cut from sheets of metal then affixed to the dial.

ASSEMBLE

To position the different parts of the movement in relation to each other. Once done entirely by hand, assembly is now very much an automated process. However, the human element has retained its importance in quality controls and inspections.

ASSORTIMENT

French term for the three parts of the escapement (escape-wheel, lever and roller).
Generally, specialist companies supply watchmakers with the lever assortment.

AXLE

A pivoted steel arbor on which the balance is mounted.

BALANCE

A circular moving part which oscillates on its rotational axis. It is coupled to the balance-spring which gives it the to-and-fro motion through which it divides time into strictly equal parts. Each to-and-fro movement ("tick-tock") is called an oscillation, and each oscillation comprises two vibrations.
A circular mass (rim) held by spokes. Combined with the spiral it forms the regulating organ of the watch.

BALANCE COCK (MODERN)

A bridge with a lug anchored to a stud. An index (or regulator) passes over a scale indicating Fast Slow in English, Avance Retard in French.

BALANCE COCK (TRADITIONAL)

Originally, in the sixteenth century, balance cocks had a simple, elongated form and were secured in their center by a key. In the eighteenth century they were decorated with elaborate chasing and engraved with animals, flowers, leaves, human heads, etc. The majority of these balance cocks could be distinguished by their form, as follows:

English, which were round with a large fastening foot. French or Continental, which were round or oval with lateral lugs for the fixing screws.

BALANCE SPRING

A very fine spring and the "heart" of a mechanical watch. Its ends are affixed to the balance and the balance cock. Its elasticity allows the balance to make regular oscillations. Its length and the balance's moment of inertia determine the duration of each oscillation. Its length can be altered to regulate the watch.

BARREL

A cylindrical box (the barrel) and toothed disc (wheel), protected by a cover. The barrel, which contains the mainspring, turns freely on its arbor. The mainspring is hooked to the barrel at its outer extremity and to the arbor at its inner extremity. The barrel wheel meshes with the first pinion of the geartrain. As it slowly rotates, its arc varies from one-ninth to one-sixth of a revolution per hour. A hanging barrel (also known as a standing barrel or floating barrel) is one whose arbor is supported at the upper end only, being attached to the barrel bridge with no support from the lower plate.

A plain barrel, used in fusee watches, has no teeth. Catgut, then a chain, is coiled round the plain barrel, connecting it to the fusee.

BARREL ARBOR

Supports the barrel and its spring. It comprises a cylinder, known as the core, and a hook to which the inner end of the mainspring is attached. The upper pivot is cut into a square for the ratchet wheel. The arbor moves in holes, one in the plate and the other in the barrel bridge.

BASIC FUNCTION

Indication of the hours, minutes and seconds using any type of display.

BEARING

A hole made directly in the brass plate and in which a steel pivot, part of the gear train or escapement, turns. The problems of friction this caused were solved when Nicolas Fatio had the idea of using drilled natural rubies as bearings. These natural stones were later replaced by synthetic rubies, made in 1892 by Auguste Verneuil.

BELL

A small, flattened bell in a clock, watch or alarm that is struck with a hammer. In a repeater watch, bells are replaced by gongs, which are strips of tempered steel, firmly secured at one end. The hours are struck on a low note; the quarter-hour is struck on two notes, one low and one high.

A chime uses three notes.

BENCH

A general term for a solid workbench used by various professions. The watchmaker's bench includes drawers for the watchmaker to keep the different tools. These drawers form a cabinet which can be separate from the bench itself.

Eighteenth-century cabinet makers used their talent to create luxurious benches that were a focal point of famous watchmakers' shops.

Today's benches are ergonomically designed and adapted to the watchmaker's different tasks, such as assembly and repairs.

BEZEL

A ring around the case middle that secures the crystal. A rotating bezel records additional information such as the duration of a given phenomenon.

The bezel on a diving watch is unidirectional. This is a deliberate feature and an additional safety factor, as the bezel rotates only in the direction that will reduce dive time. Hence if the bezel is accidentally turned, the diver can still surface with sufficient air and respect decompression stops.

BLOCK

In a lever escapement, the dart is fixed to a block at the base of the fork.

BOLT

A catch that can be operated from the outside of a watch case to trigger a mechanism, for example to set the hands.

BOTTOM PLATE

The plate that bears the various movement parts and in particular the bridges. The dial is usually affixed to the bottom side of the plate. The plate is pierced with holes for the screws and recesses for the jewels in which the pivots of the movement wheels will run.

BOW

Variously shaped ring for suspending a pocket watch and fastening a chain.

BRIDGE

A metal plate under which the pivots of the wheels and pinions turn.
Both ends of the bridge are secured to the plate by screws. Generally a bridge is named according to its function, e.g. center-wheel bridge, barrel bridge, balance cock, etc.

BURNISH

To polish the pivots using a burnisher (polishing tool).

CABINET

A small workshop in eighteenth or nineteenth-century Geneva, on the top floor of a house where there was the most natural light.

CABINOTIER

In Geneva, a workman employed by a cabinet. A cabinotier was not necessarily a watchmaker. He could be a jeweler, engraver, stonecutter, etc., provided he worked for a cabinet and was employed in watchmaking.

CALIBER

Synonym of size. Sully used this term c. 1715 to denote the layout and dimensions of the different movement pillars, wheels, barrel, etc. Since then caliber has been used to indicate the shape of the movement, its bridges, the origin of the watch, its maker's name, etc.
It now designates the movement itself.
The round caliber is the most commonly encountered. It is described in terms of its casing diameter, measured in lignes or millimetres, for example a 10''' / 22.5 mm round caliber. The shape and layout of the bridges are used to distinguish between a bridge caliber, in which each part of the train has a bridge; the revolver caliber, whose barrel bridge bears a slight resemblance to a pistol; the curved bridge caliber, where the bridges curve towards the center of the movement; and the three-quarter-plate caliber, in which the entire train except for the escape wheel is fitted under a bridge that covers some three-quarters of the movement.

CAM

A part that is profiled to transform or modify motion. For example, a cam is used to reset the chronograph hand or activate the hammers in a minute-repeater.

CANNON PINION

A friction-fit pinion, part of the motion work, that carries the minute hand.

CENTURY LEAP YEAR

Introduced with the reform of the Gregorian calendar in 1582 to take into account the time taken for the earth to make one complete revolution of the sun, i.e. 365.2422 days. A century year is a leap year every 400 years, i.e. for a century year to be a leap year, it must be divisible by 400.

CHAMFER (BEVEL)

To form a flat surface by hand-filing the sharp edge of a bridge, plate, screw head, etc. Chamfering is a distinguishing feature of a superior quality watch.

CHIMES

The quarter-hours are sounded on three, four or more gongs with different pitches, the best-known being the Westminster chimes.

CHRONOGRAPH

A watch indicating hours, minutes and seconds combined with a mechanism whose hand can be started, stopped and returned to zero on demand to measure a duration to one-fifth, -tenth or even one-hundredth of a second. Subcounters for the minutes and hours (usually 30 minutes and 12 hours) totalize the number of revolutions by the chronograph hand. The accuracy of these recorded times can be guaranteed only if the chronograph has satisfied the criteria of the chronometer label.

The first chronographs deposited drops of ink on their dial; this no longer being the case, strictly speaking a chronograph should be called a chronoscope.

CHRONOMETER (GENERAL DEFINITION)

A chronometer is, etymologically, an instrument for measuring the time. With usage it has come to mean a high-precision watch displaying seconds whose movement has been controlled over a period of several days, in different positions and at different temperatures, by an official neutral body. Only mechanisms that have satisfied the criteria for precision of ISO 3159, or its equivalent, are issued with an official chronometer certificate.

In Switzerland, the Contrôle Officiel Suisse des Chronomètres (COSC) has the power to award these certificates. Based on the requirements of ISO 3159, the COSC has also drawn up a set of specifications for the testing of quartz movements.

While a chronograph can be used to measure an interval of time, it can only use the name chronometer if it has been officially certified as such.

CHUCK

An important workbench tool for holding small parts to be shaped or filed.

CLEPSYDRA

Also known as a water clock. An instrument that measures time by the flow of a quantity of a fluid (water or mercury).

The Egyptians and the Chinese used clepsydras in the fifteenth-century BCE. Clepsydras were also still used in the eighteenth century. Improvements were made to the system by incorporating a cylindrical float chamber that moved a hand around a dial, marked into hours. Famous clepsydras include one, now vanished, by Ctesibius, a copy of that can be seen at the Munich Science Museum, and the one that Harun al-Rashid gave to Charlemagne in 809.

CLUTCH

A coupling that temporarily connects two rotating parts, one driving and one driven.

In a chronograph mechanism, the clutch temporarily connects two wheels. One wheel transfers power from the mainspring to the other.

Depending on its position on the winding stem, the sliding pinion transfers power from the rotating of the crown to the mainspring when winding; to the hand gear train when setting the time.

COAXIAL

Having coincident axes or mounted on concentric shafts, for example the hour and minute hands, and possibly the seconds hands.

COLUMN WHEEL

The wheel which coordinates the start, stop and return to zero functions of the chronograph hand.

In a standard quality chronograph, the column wheel is replaced by a system of cames.

CONTRÔLE OFFICIEL SUISSE DES CHRONOMÈTRES (COSC)

The COSC awards the title of chronometer to each watch whose accuracy and consistency of rate has been demonstrated over fifteen days of tests at one of the COSC's Bureaux Officiels (BO). Each watch is tested in five positions and at different temperatures. The COSC is a non-profit association set up by five swiss cantons, Bern, Geneva, Neuchâtel, Soleure, and Vaud. Its headquarters are in La Chaux-de-Fonds. The BO are in Biel, Geneva and Le Locle. A certificate is issued to an individual watch, not to a model or a range.

CÔTES OR VAGUES DE GENÈVE

A decoration of undulating lines, like waves, frequently used to embellish superior-quality movements.

COUNT WHEEL (LOCKING PLATE)

A wheel with alternating notches and raised portions that controls the number of hours struck.

COUNTDOWN TIMER

A device for counting backwards over a given interval.

CUVETTE

A second cover inside a watch case back, often engraved with inscriptions or the maker's signature, which provides additional protection against dust.

DATE

The number, in order, of each day in the month.

DEAD SECONDS

A hand that jumps forward when a second has elapsed. Breguet used the expression *seconde d'un coup* or "sudden second". Generally the jump of a hand is a distinctive feature of a quartz watch.
In mechanical watchmaking this "function" is a technical feat.

DECIMAL (REVOLUTIONARY) (REPUBLICAN)

A watch or clock dial made in 1793, after the French Revolution had imposed the decimal calendar. The year was divided into 12 months and each month into three 10-day periods known as *décades*. The day was divided into 10 hours and each hour into 100 minutes. The decimal or Republican dial was therefore graduated from 1 to 10. Never fully accepted, manufacture of these dials ceased in 1795.

DETENT

A lever that restrains then releases a mechanism and in doing so regulates its movement.

DIRECT-DRIVE SECONDS (TROTTEUSE)

A hand that moves forward in small jumps, each of which corresponds to one vibration of the balance. A distinctive feature of a mechanical watch indicating the seconds.

DISC

A flat, thin, round plate. The calendar disc rotates under the dial; its indications are shown through an aperture. Other discs display the day, month or moon phase.

DRUM

Lateral wall of a barrel or other similar hollow, cylindrical part.
The inside of the barrel drum is fitted with a hook to take the mainspring.

DUAL TIME ZONE

Describes a watch that simultaneously gives the time in two time zones, usually local and the wearer's home.

EBAUCHE

An unfinished movement sold as such. Until around 1850, an *ébauche* comprised only the plate, bridges, fusee and barrel. It was known as a blanc and was finished at the *établissage*.
The modern *ébauche* is a watch movement, with or without jewels but always without its regulating organ, mainspring, dial and hands. It is also known as a *blanc roulant*.

ENDSTONE

An undrilled jewel that cushions the pivot of the balance staff.

ENGINE-TURNING (GUILLOCHÉ)

A style of hand or machine engraving with intersecting wavy or straight lines. When the piece is moved horizontally or vertically against the tool, the finished effect is guilloché, compared with flinqué or flinking which follows a radial movement.

ENGRAVING

The art of forming patterns either by hand, using a graver, or by machine such as a rose engine.

EQUATION OF TIME

The equation of time is the difference between true solar time and mean time. True solar time, given by sundials, varies from day to day because of the earth's elliptical orbit, and according to the longitude of the point of observation.

Mean time, given by watches, ignores these variations and for every day of the year mathematically divides time into equal hours. Four times a year, on April 15, June 14, September 1 and December 24, true solar time and mean time coincide. On the other days, the difference ranges from minus 16 minutes and 23 seconds on November 4, to plus 14 minutes and 22 seconds on February 11.

In 2000, Audemars Piguet unveiled an equation of time watch which combines the equation of time, sunrise, sunset and perpetual calendar. The equation of time hand clearly indicates this daily difference.

ESCAPEMENT

A mechanism that is fitted between the gears and the regulating organ. Its function is to suspend the gears' motion at regular intervals and to supply energy to the balance.

The main types of watch escapement are: recoil escapements (verge or crown wheel), dead-beat escapements (cylinder, virgule, double virgule) detached escapements (lever, detent).

The lever escapement is by far the most common today. Exceptional watches may be fitted with a different kind, often a detent or virgule escapement. In terms of escapements, we may historically speak of the lever and indeed the Swiss lever type, given that the Swiss lever escapement is the most widely used today because it is especially suited to watches and chronometers.

ETABLISSAGE

A procedure for manufacturing the watch and/or movement by assembling the various parts. As a general rule, the procedure in full comprises taking delivery of, inspecting and stocking the *ébauches*, the components for the movement and exterior; assembly; timing; fitting the dial and hands; fitting the movement, and the final inspection before packaging and dispatching.

ETABLISSEUR

In Switzerland, a watchmaker who buys *ébauches* and parts in order to assemble them.

EXTERIOR

The different parts (case, dial, hands, crystal, crown, etc.) that help to give the watch its finished and functional appearance.

FABRIQUE

A term formerly used in Geneva to describe all the different professions involved in watchmaking.

FINISHING (FINISSAGE)

The final operation in a process. On a watch case, the last stage in assembling the parts so that they function.

FINISSEUR

Generally speaking, a skilled worker who performs the last stage in a process, for example who finishes a watch case or dial, or who fits the gear train. The finisseur used to round off the wheels and correct any defects to the gears.

FLANGE

The part inside a watch case that supports the movement.

FLY-BACK (RETOUR EN VOL)

A function of particular use to pilots, by which the chronograph hand can be reset to zero and immediately started again by pressing once on the pushpiece.

The operation of stopping, returning to zero and restarting the hand in three separate movements would be too time-consuming at high speed.

FORK

In clocks and watches, an extension of the lever that connects the escapement and the pendulum rod or balance.

FOUDROYANTE (JUMPING SECONDS OR HAND) (FLYING SECONDS)

On a chronograph, a hand that makes one rotation every second, pausing four, five, even eight times to indicate quarters, fifths or eighths of a second.

FREQUENCY

The number of oscillations per second, measured in Hertz. The balance makes a to-and-fro movement at a given frequency (two vibrations). The higher the frequency, the more accurate the watch: 21,600 vibrations/hour (3 Hz), 28,800 vibrations/hour (4 Hz) and 36,000 vibrations/hour (5 Hz).

FUSEE

A more or less conical part with spiral grooves for gut, and after around 1640 chain, which connects to the barrel. It regulates the power transferred to the gears. Almost all sixteenth-, seventeenth- and eighteenth-century watches have a fusee.

GEAR TRAIN

A system for transmitting power and motion through toothed wheels. In a watch, the train comprises a wheel whose teeth mesh with a pinion's leaves.

GEARS

A set of wheels and pinions whereby the movement of one sets all the others in motion. There are different types of gears, e.g. winding gears, strike-train, etc.

GONG

In a movement and struck by hammers, gongs replaced bells in striking watches in the early nineteenth century, allowing for much thinner watches.

GRANDE SONNERIE

Watch that strikes the hours and quarters in passing and repeats the hour at each quarter.
The hour and quarter strikes can be repeated on demand.
Certain grande sonnerie mechanisms are combined with a minute-repeater which repeats hours, quarters and minutes on demand.

GREGORIAN CALENDAR

The calendar now adopted by the majority of countries, introduced in 1582 by Pope Gregory XIII in his reform of the Julian calendar. With its 365.25 days, the Julian year was 11 minutes and 14 seconds longer than the interval between two consecutive spring equinoxes. Because of the difference accumulated over the centuries, by 1582 it was 10 days out.
To solve this problem, Gregory XIII took ten days from the calendar: Thursday October 4, 1582 was followed by Friday October 15. As previously, every fourth year became a leap year by adding a 29th day to February.
In order to erase three days every 400 years, a century year was no longer a leap year except when divisible by 400. Hence 1600 and 2000 were both leap years whereas 1700, 1800 and 1900 were ordinary years, as will be 2100 and 2400.
The Gregorian calendar is therefore just three days in advance every 10,000 years.

HAMMER

A metal part that strikes gongs, causing them to vibrate and produce sound.

HAND-SETTING

The action of adjusting the hands of a watch to the time shown on a reference clock.

HERTZ (HZ)

A unit of frequency of a periodic phenomenon equal to one cycle per second.

HOUR-WHEEL

The wheel that carries the hour hand.

HUNTER

A watch whose case has a front and back cover.

IMPULSE

Movement transmitted by a mechanical part. In a lever escapement, the impulse occurs via the impulse surface of the wheel tooth and the pallet.

INDEX (REGULATOR)

A device for adjusting a watch's rate by increasing or reducing the effective length of the balance spring. The index is a steel lever, the shorter end of which carries the curb pins which embrace the spring, and the longer end of which passes over a scale marked in French A and R (avance and retard) or in English F and S (fast and slow). The index is friction-fitted on the balance's endpiece. The watch is regulated by moving the index forwards; the result of this can be gauged from the graduations on the balance cock.

INDICATOR

The indicators of a watch are its dial and hands.

INERTIA BLOCK

Small pieces of metal placed on the balance of the watches to regulate variation in rate in the absence of an index, in particular for chronometers.
A small piece of metal whose inertia slows or accelerates the movement of the balance.

INTERMEDIATE WHEEL

A small toothed wheel, part of the hand-setting mechanism.

INVERTED CALIBER

Caliber whose dial is on the same side as the bridges and gear train rather than on the bottom-plate side.

ISOCHRONAL (ISOCHRONOUS)

Recurring at regular intervals. The oscillations of a pendulum or balance are isochronal when their duration is the same regardless of their amplitude.

ISOCHRONISM

The property of being isochronal. The science of timing lies in achieving isochronism of the regulating organ of a timekeeping instrument. The principal factors that can impair a balance's isochronism are the escapement, incorrect poising of the balance and spring, play between the curb pins and the balance spring, centrifugal force and magnetic fields.

JUMPING HOUR

A means of display in which the hour, shown through an aperture, instantly changes every 60 minutes.

JUMPING SECONDS

On a chronograph, a hand that makes one rotation every second, pausing four, five, even eight times to indicate quarters, fifths or eighths of a second. Also called foudroyante.

LARGE DATE

A date function with large numerals on two independent discs, displayed through oversized apertures.

LEAP YEAR

Introduced by Julius Caesar in 45 BCE as part of the Julian calendar, the leap year was already found in certain Egyptian and Babylonian calendars.
It has 366 days and generally occurs every four years; to take into account the time taken for the earth to make one complete revolution of the sun, i.e. 365.2422 days.

LEAP YEAR CALENDAR

The leap year calendar takes automatically into account months with fewer than 31 days and February when it has counts 28 days. It must be adjusted every fourth year.

LÉPINE CALIBER (MOVEMENT)

Jean-Antoine Lépine (1720–1814) was a French watchmaker and inventor of the caliber that bears his name. Its principal characteristic is that it dispensed with the fusee and replaced the top plate and pillars with bridges. This made room for the balance inside rather than on top of the mechanism. The result was a much thinner movement. In a pocket watch, the Lépine or open-face caliber denotes a structure in which the seconds hand is in line with the winding-stem, as opposed to the hunter caliber in which the seconds hand is on an axis from 3 to 9 o'clock, at right angles to the winding-stem.

LÉPINE WATCH (OPEN-FACE)

In a pocket watch, a structure in which the seconds hand is positioned in line with the winding stem, as opposed to the hunter caliber in which the seconds hand is at right angles to the winding stem, at 6 and 3 o'clock respectively.

LEVER

Part of a watch or clock escapement, made in steel or brass.
The lever, whose form suggests a ship's anchor, has a dual function: it transmits energy from the spring via the wheels to the balance in order to maintain its oscillations. It also controls the movement of the wound gears.

LEVER HÉLIAQUE D'UN ASTRE

An annual occurrence which marks the end of a period of invisibility that began with the star's heliacal setting due to conjunction with the rising sun.

LIGNE

Also *ligne parisienne*. An old unit of measurement in traditional watchmaking, prior to the metric system and directly inherited from the French pied (foot) under the Ancien *Régime*. *One ligne equals 2.2558 mm, rounded up to 2.26 mm. A foot (‹) measured 12* inches *of 12 lignes (‘) each.* The usual abbreviation is a triple apostrophe (‴) after the figure. Hence a movement can be described as having a diameter of 11‴ or 11 lignes, which is 24.8 mm.

LUNATION

The period of time elapsing between two successive new moons.

MALTESE CROSS

A device to prevent overwinding, comprising a finger fixed to the barrel arbor and a small wheel in the shape of a Maltese cross, mounted on the barrel cover. The Maltese cross is also the symbol of Vacheron Constantin.

MANUAL

Describes a movement that is wound by hand using the winding crown.

MARINE CHRONOMETER

Traditionally, marine chronometer refers to a large watch for keeping time onboard ship. In the latter years of the eighteenth century, the term was extended to mean a timepiece that is:
— almost always with a detent escapement;
— whose direct-drive seconds hand jumps forward every half-second;
— hung in gimbals so as to maintain a horizontal position regardless of the ship's movements;
— usually with a power reserve indicator;
— protected from knocks and damp by a wooden (generally mahogany) case.
This precision instrument's main function is to determine longitude at sea. When the ship leaves port, its chronometer is set to Greenwich Mean Time. The ship also carries special tables (e.g. *Connaissance des Temps*, Nautical Almanac) which indicate, for each day of the year, the time at which the sun and certain stars cross the Greenwich meridian. To determine the ship's longitude, the appointed officer consults the chronometer to note the time at which the sun or a star crosses the ship's meridian. The difference between this time and the time given in the tables at which the same star or the sun crosses the Greenwich meridian indicates the longitude of the point of observation east or west of Greenwich.
Ships also use smaller watches known as ships' chronometers or deck watches.

MARKER

A symbol that replaces some or all of the numerals on a dial.

MOON PHASE

The time between successive new moons, shown on a watch dial from 1 to 29 ½ days, corresponding to the period of lunar revolution around the earth.

MOON PHASES

A mechanism and display representing the different phases of the moon. A complete lunation takes 29 days, 12 hours, 44 minutes and 2.8 seconds and is divided into four phases. These are new moon, first quarter, full moon, and last quarter.

MOTION WORK

The gears under the dial that transfer the rotation of the cannon pinion to the hour wheel.

MOVEMENT

The duly assembled organs and mechanisms of a watch, meaning the winding and hand-setting mechanism, the mainspring, the gears, the escapement and the regulating organ (spring balance).
Anatomically speaking, the movement comprises the *ébauche*, the regulating parts and other components (springs, jewels, pivots, pinions, screws, shock-absorbers, etc.).

OBSERVATORY CHRONOMETER

A chronometer that has received an official rating certificate from an observatory.

OIGNON (WATCH)

A style of watch made in France in the late seventeenth and early eighteenth centuries, its fat, bulbous form suggesting an onion. Most oignon watches featured a chased brass case, very occasionally in silver and on very rare occasions gold. In later centuries, oignon became a familiar and ironic term to describe a large, thick watch.

OSCILLATING PINION

The oscillating pinion, which comprises a mobile stem and two pinions, allows the chronograph to function very efficiently by replacing the two large wheels of the anterior movements. A coupling system enables the chronograph to locate onto the watch movement with ultimate precision. The chronograph's lightning-fast start — an incredible 2/1,000th of a second — guarantees the utmost in timekeeping accuracy.

OSCILLATING WEIGHT (ROTOR)

In a self-winding movement, a heavy metal disc that turns freely in both directions to wind the mainspring.

OSCILLATOR

A device such as a pendulum or balance that produces the oscillations that divide time into equal units: a balance spring in a mechanical watch; a quartz in a quartz watch.

PAIRING

The action of coupling a spring with its balance.

PALLET

In a lever escapement, a small parallelepiped of ruby, sapphire or garnet, set in each of the lever's arms; one is the entrance pallet and one is the exit pallet.

PANTOGRAPH

An instrument for copying designs on an identical, reduced or enlarged scale. In 1841, Georges-Auguste Leschot began working with a pantograph at Vacheron Constantin. It used a matrix or pattern to punch-mark and mill identical watch plates. This technique was the first step towards interchangeable movement parts.

PAWL (CLICK)

A lever with a "beak" which when activated by a spring engages with the teeth of a wheel usually to allow the wheel to turn in one direction only.

PENDANT

The part of a pocket watch that is fixed to the case middle. The different parts of the pendant are the pipe, the head and the neck. The foot is the invisible part that is soldered inside the case. After the mid-nineteenth century, the pendant, crown and bow formed a whole whose shape and size were designed to complement the case. In a wristwatch, the pendant is reduced to a small cylindrical stem on which the winding crown turns. Pendant or keyless winding is by means of the crown, as opposed to the winding system on early pocket watches by means of a key or pushbutton.

PENDULUM

A heavy body suspended from a fixed point from which it can swing freely to and fro. A clock pendulum comprises the suspension, which can be a spring, knife-edge or wire, the generally cylindrical metal or wood rod, and the bob, which is the weight at the end of the rod. Galileo used a pendulum in his astronomical observations in 1595. Huygens expanded on Galileo's theory to build his pendulum clock in 1657. It was a further twenty years or so before his invention reached the Jura, where the Mayet brothers, both blacksmiths, applied it to what appears to be the ancestor of the Comtois clock.

PERIOD

An interval of time defined by the regular and repeated occurrence of a given phenomenon.

PERPETUAL CALENDAR

Devised to incorporate the specificities of the Gregorian calendar, it is perpetual because it automatically adjusts to months with 30 days and to the 28 or 29 days in February. To do this, it incorporates a mechanical memory whose sequences are repeated every 48 months to correspond to the cycle of leap years. It need only be adjusted for exceptional non-leap year years, the next being 2100 and 2400.

PERPETUAL CALENDAR (WATCH)

A watch whose perpetual calendar automatically takes the number of days in the month into account: 30 or 31 and the 28 or 29 days of February for ordinary and leap years. Unless it takes into account century years that are not leap years, it will need adjusting in 2100, 2200 and 2300 but not in 2400. A 48-month dial, derived from pocket watches, corresponds to three ordinary years and one leap year. On the more legible 12-month dial, ordinary and leap years are shown by a hand or aperture.

Some perpetual calendars can include the following additional functions:

Week number, this being virtually the same as the interval between two consecutive phases of the moon (see complication).

Year corresponding to the order of years in a religious era, whether Christian or another faith (see complication).

Sunrise and sunset for a given location (see complication); when a perpetual calendar mechanism drives the sunrise and sunset wheels, these indications are said to be perpetual.

Sidereal hour equal to one-twenty-fourth of the sidereal day (see complication), this being the interval between two successive transits of a star over the meridian.

Exceptional watches can give other astronomical indications such as the declination of the sun (angular distance north or south from the celestial equator), the apparent movement of the planets, the line of node to forecast eclipses, a star chart for a given location, etc.

PETITE SONNERIE

Watch that strikes the hours and quarters in passing without repeating the hours at each quarter.

The hour and quarter strikes can be repeated on demand if the subsidiary seconds are coupled to a striking mechanism.

PINION

A watch part, generally with 6 to 14 leaves (teeth). The different parts of the pinion are the leaves, the seat to which the wheel is riveted, the shank and the pivots.

PIVOT

A part that runs in a fixed support (bearing).

POINÇON DE GENÈVE (HALLMARK OF GENEVA)

A distinctive seal depicting the Geneva coat of arms, granted by an official body at the Ecole d'Horlogerie de Genève and placed on watches whose quality and finish conform to precise specifications. Created in 1886 by the canton of Geneva.

POLISH

To give a smooth and shiny finish, e.g. mirror polish (or black polish).

POWER RESERVE, INDICATOR

The time the watch will continue to function before the mainspring must be wound.

PULSOMETER

A chronograph or sports counter whose dial includes a pulsometric scale to measure the number of heartbeats per minute. Usually calibrated for 15 or 30 beats, the hand is stopped at the patient's 15th or 30th heartbeat; the dial indicates the frequency per minute.

PUSH-BUTTON

A button that commands a function, for example to open a case cover or to start and stop a chronograph.

RACK

A toothed segment used in certain passing strike mechanisms that do not have a count wheel (locking plate).

RAILROAD

A minute scale on a dial that resembles a railway track.

RATE

The functioning of a timepiece evaluated in terms of its regularity. Daily rate is the amount of time a watch gains or loses over 24 hours compared with a reference time.

REGULATING ORGAN (REGULATOR)

The regulating organs in a mechanical watch are the balance and spring whose function is to count time. A clock's regulating organ is its pendulum. In an electronic watch it can be a motor or a resonator (tuning fork or quartz crystal).

REPAIR

To restore a watch to a functioning state.

REPASSAGE

The final and complete inspection of the watch with its mechanism and aesthetics, just before it leaves the manufacturer. Both rate and appearance are inspected.

REPEATER

A watch that strikes the hour on demand by activating a pushpiece or a slide (bolt). There are several types of repeater.

Half-quarter and quarter repeater:
This watch, which first appeared in England around 1675, strikes the quarter-hour and on demand. Credit for its invention must be shared between Edward Barlow, Thomas Tompion and Daniel Quare, who was granted a patent in 1687. The quarter repeater watch strikes the quarter-hour on demand and on two notes. The half-quarter repeater strikes a high tone to signal when the following half-quarter has passed.

Five-minute repeater:
This system strikes the hour, quarter-hour and five-minute intervals on two tones, meaning these two notes can be heard up to eleven times in an hour.

Minute repeater:
The first mechanisms to precisely indicate the number of minutes elapsed appeared in the first decade of the eighteenth century, for the most part in southern Germany. Thomas Mudge has traditionally been credited with the invention of this complication, around 1750.

COMPLICATION STRIKES

These mechanisms strike the hour and/or the quarter-hour either automatically ("passing strike") or on demand by means of a pushpiece or slide. Naturally, watchmakers have dreamed up even more complex mechanisms. The grande sonnerie automatically strikes both the hours and quarters at each quarter, and repeats the hours, quarters and minutes on demand. Sometimes it combines with its "little sister", the petite sonnerie which sounds the hours and the quarters without repeating the hours at every quarter. The mechanism can be silenced using an "all or nothing" or "silent" slide.

Even after the invention of safety matches in 1845 made it possible to consult the time by the light of a candle or oil lamp, master watchmakers have continued to rise to the challenge of the minute repeater mechanism.

RETROGRADE

An hour, minute, seconds or calendar hand which moves across a scale and, at the end of its cycle, returns immediately to zero to begin again.

REVOLUTIONARY CALENDAR

A decree of October 5, 1793, promulgated on November 24 of the same year, introduced the French Revolutionary (or Republican) calendar, based on the decimal system. It was declared to begin retroactively on September 22, 1792, the day the Republic was proclaimed and the autumn equinox. The year was divided into twelve months, each with three ten-day weeks or *décades*, in compliance with the metric system. Five additional days (six in a leap year) were placed at the end of the year. The same also imposed the decimal hour. Henceforth the twenty-four hour day was divided into ten hours, each with 100 minutes and each minute having 100 seconds. A decree of February 9, 1794 launched a competition inviting scholars and clockmakers to provide practical solutions to this new decimal time. However, very few sundials, watches or clocks were made to this new standard. The decimal hour was never really adopted, and was suspended for an indefinite period on April 7, 1795. Napoleon I signed the decree by which the Revolutionary calendar was abandoned on January 1, 1806. It was briefly reinstated by the *Journal Officiel* during the 1871 Commune.

RIM

A circular mass held by spokes to form the balance.

RUBY

A very hard red stone that is a type of corundum (aluminum oxide). Ruby is especially suited to making bearings (jewels) for the watch's different moving parts and the organs of the escapement, thereby reducing friction to a minimum.

Drilled rubies were used for the first time by Nicholas Facio de Duillier in 1704. Watches today use synthetic rubies known as jewels. Drilled and polished, they are used as bearings for the different pivots to minimize friction and wear. As a general rule, a simple mechanical watch, i.e. one that indicates hours, minutes and seconds, should have at least fifteen jewels at the points most exposed to friction.

SAFETY ROLLER

In a lever escapement, a disc that limits movement of the fork.

SECRET SPRING

A spring that releases the cover on a hunter watch case.

SECULAR PERPETUAL CALENDAR

Devised to incorporate the specificities of the Gregorian calendar, it is perpetual because it automatically adjusts to months with 30 days and to the 28 or 29 days in February. Unlike the perpetual calendar, it is also automatically adjusted for exceptional non-leap year years, the next being 2100 and 2200.

SELF-WINDING (AUTOMATIC)

Describes a mechanism that winds the mainspring by using the movement of the arm to cause a rotor to rotate, and which, via specific gears, winds the mainspring.

SIDEREAL DAY

A unit of time used by astronomers, defined as the

interval of time taken by a star to make two successive upper meridian transits.

SILENT

A manually operated means of silencing a striking mechanism equipped with this function.

SIMPLE CALENDAR (WATCH)

A simple calendar shows the date, i.e. the number, in order, of each day in the month. Certain simple calendars also display the names of the months. A simple calendar mechanism uses a single disc display, or two discs when it incorporates a large date function. A full calendar shows the date, the day of the week, the month and moon phases (new and full moons separated by the first and last quarters).

A complete calendar mechanism uses three discs, four discs when it incorporates a large date function, and four when moon phases are added. Whether full or partial, a simple calendar does not automatically take months with fewer than 31 days into account, or leap years, and must therefore be adjusted five times a year. Information is displayed in letters and digits, or just digits, through one or more apertures, or by means of hands.

SKELETON MOVEMENT

A movement whose plate and bridges have been cut away to expose the wheels, leaving only the substance the watch needs to function. The movement is placed between two sapphire crystals to be seen.

SLIDE

In a repeater watch, a part made from the same metal as the case and which slides along the case middle to wind the spring of the striking mechanism.
A silent slide prevents the mechanism from striking.

SPLIT-SECONDS (CHRONOGRAPH)

The split-seconds chronograph is used to time different events that begin but do not end together. When set, the hand of the chronograph and the hand of the split seconds button when the first event ends.

After reading the intermediate time a second push on the button makes it catch up with the first hand and the two continue their movement together. At the end of the second event, the split-seconds hand is stopped again to read this second intermediate time, and so on. At the end of the last observed event, both hands can be stopped and returned to zero. One pushpiece operates the split-seconds hand only while the second pushpiece operates both hands.

SPRING

The source of mechanical energy in a watch. A strip of tempered blued steel or a special steel alloy, coiled inside the barrel.

STAMPING PRESS

A high-precision tool that revolutionized mechanized watch production, used to shear, bend, shape, pierce and adjust most of the parts of the watch.

STIPPLING (SPOTTING)

A decorative finish of overlapping circles in a close-set concentric pattern that gives a distinctive textured effect.

STONE

In watchmaking, a precious stone used as a bearing, endstone or pallet-stone, known internationally as jewels.
The majority of stones (jewels) used in watches today are synthetic. Their role is to minimize friction.

STOPWORK

System that controls tension to the mainspring when wound. The best-known stopwork mechanism is the Maltese cross.

STRIKING MECHANISM

An acoustic device that automatically or on demand indicates the hour, and possibly quarter-hour and minutes, or sounds at a pre-set time. There are different striking mechanisms: passing strike, quarter repeater, minute repeater, petite sonnerie, grande sonnerie, alarm.

STUD

Pins the outer end of the spiral to the balance-cock, either directly or using a mobile stud-holder.

SUBSIDIARY SECONDS

As opposed to center or sweep seconds, a small subdial showing seconds, generally at 6 o'clock.

SUNRISE AND SUNSET

Period between the rising and setting of the sun. A 24-hour interval, determined by the earth's rotation on its axis.

SWEEP SECONDS

Also called center seconds. A seconds hand positioned at the center of the main dial.

TACHYMETER

An instrument for measuring speed. In watchmaking, a chronograph or sports counter with a scale for reading speed in kilometres per hour (kph) or another unit.

TERMINAGE

The assembly and inspection of all the watch's parts.

TIME ZONE

In order to standardize time measurement in each country, since 1883 the earth has been divided into twenty-four time zones, the first of which is intersected by the Greenwich meridian, which is the prime or zero meridian. Each point within a given time zone has the same legal time.

TOOTH

A projection on the edge of a gear, escapement wheel, ratchet wheel, etc.

TOURBILLON

A system devised and patented by Abraham-Louis Breguet in 1801 to compensate for errors of rate caused by the earth's gravitational force in upright positions. The escapement is mounted in a revolving cage with the regulating organ (balance) at the center.

The escape-wheel pinion turns around the fixed fourth wheel. The cage generally revolves once a minute and, in doing so, compensates for errors of rate caused by the vertical position in which pocket watches spend most of their time. This delicate and complex structure is one of watchmaking's most ingenious mechanisms. A simplified and more robust alternative is the karussel, where the cage is driven not by the fourth wheel but by the third wheel. A tourbillon may contain a lever or a detent escapement.

TRAIN

In a watch, the wheels and pinions.
In a simple watch, the going train comprises the barrel, the center pinion, the center wheel, the third wheel and pinion, the fourth wheel and pinion and the escape wheel pinion. The motion work comprises the cannon pinion, the minute wheel and pinion and the hour wheel.

TROTTEUSE

A seconds hand, mounted either in the center of the main dial or in a subsidiary dial.

UNDER-DIAL WORK

Collective term for the mechanisms, such as for striking, calendar or motionwork, between the dial and the dial plate.

UNIVERSAL HOUR

One twenty-fourth of the universal day which begins at midnight at the Prime Meridian at Greenwich. Following the 1884 International Meridian Conference in Washington, the earth was divided into twenty-four time zones, each covering 15 degrees longitude measured from the Greenwich meridian. Subsequently, universal time replaced the multiple times based on local meridians. Until 1911, France continued to use the Paris meridian as the basis for its time.

UNIVERSAL TIME (UT)

Since 1972, a continuation of Greenwich Mean Time (GMT) which is mean solar time at the Greenwich

meridian. Universal Time (UT) is a measurement
of time based on the earth's rotation. It is therefore
influenced by irregularities due, among other factors,
to the tides produced by the sun and moon.
There are several Universal Times, one of the most
important being Coordinated Universal Time (UTC).
This international standard is the basis of civil time.
It is derived from International Atomic Time (TAI),
itself based on the atomic definition of the second and
measured using a series of atomic clocks.

VANE

Uses air friction to slow a moving part, for example
the arm on a gravity escapement.

VIBRATION

Movement of a pendulum or oscillating body between
two extreme positions.
The balance of a mechanical watch generally makes
five vibrations per second, equivalent to 18,000
vibrations/hour (2.5 Hz). A more accurate mechanical
watch makes 10 vibrations per second or 36,000
vibrations/hour (5Hz). A quartz watch makes 64,000
vibrations per second (32 MHz).
An oscillation ("tick-tock") equals two vibrations
(although the term oscillation is sometimes incorrectly
used to refer to a vibration).

WHEEL

A circular component that rotates around an axis and
whose function is to transmit power or motion.

WIND

The action of tightening the mainspring coiled inside
the barrel, by means of the winding crown (in a hand-
wound watch) or the rotor (in a self-winding watch).

WINDING MECHANISM

The mechanism that tightens the mainspring in a
watch or lifts the weights in a clock. It comprises
about ten parts.
The winding and hand-setting mechanisms nowadays
have some parts in common.

WORLD TIME

Describes a watch that indicates, usually by means
of subdials surrounding the main dial, local time
(true solar time) in different world cities. Often these
cities were chosen for their political or economic
importance prior to 1883, when Universal Time was
introduced.

BIBLIOGRAPHY

WORKS ON VACHERON CONSTANTIN

Annales de la maison d'Horlogerie Vacheron et Constantin
Charles Constantin

Les Maîtres des Heures
Vacheron Constantin, 1955

L'Univers de Vacheron Constantin,
Lausanne - Geneva.
C. Lambelet / L. Coen
Scriptar SA/Vacheron Constantin,
1992

Vacheron Constantin
Franco Cologni
Assouline, Paris, 2000

*Treasures of Vacheron Constantin:
A Legacy of Watchmaking since 1775*
Julien Marchenoir
Hazan, 2011

Vacheron Constantin: Artist of Time
Franco Cologni, photography by
Bruno Ehrs
Flammarion, Paris 2015

**WORKS ON THE HISTORY,
TECHNIQUES AND ART OF
WATCHMAKING**

*Wristwatches: History of a Century's
Development*
H. Kahlert / R. Mühe / G.L. Brunner
Schiffer Publishing, 1986

*Revolution in Time: Clocks and the
Making of the Modern World*
D.S. Landes Harvard University Press,
1983

*Dictionnaire professionnel illustré
de l'Horlogerie*
G. A. Berner Chambre Suisse de
l'horlogerie à la Chaux-de-Fonds, new
edition 1988

*L'économie genevoise de la Réforme à la
fin de l'Ancien Régime*
Liliane Mottu-Weber, Anne-Marie
Piuz, Liliane Mottu-Weber et al.
Georg et Société d'histoire et
d'archéologie de Genève, Geneva, 1990

*L'Homme et le Temps en Suisse 1291-
1991,* Institut l'Homme et le Temps, La
Chaux-de-Fonds, 1991

Arts et technique de la montre
E. Introna / G. Ribolini
Du May, Boulogne, 1993

Révolution inachevée, révolution oubliée,
David Hiler and Bernard Lescaze
Suzanne Hurter, Geneva, 1992

*Comment habiller le Temps. Un siècle de
Design horloger - JUVENIA,*
Lausanne - La Chaux-de-Fonds
H. Marquis.
Éditions Scriptar SA/Juvenia, 1995

*The Mastery of Time: A History of
Timekeeping, from the Sundial to the
Wristwatch*
Dominique Fléchon, Franco Cologni
Flammarion, Paris, 2011

**WORKS ON CIVILIZATIONS AND
CALENDARS**

Histoire du calendrier romain
François Blondel
Paris, 1682

On Judaism
Martin Buber
Schocken Books, new edition 2016

Histoire des Mœurs,
Encyclopédie de la Pléiade, Gallimard,
Paris, 1990

*Clepsydra: Essay on the Plurality of Time
in Judaism*
Sylvie-Anne Goldberg, translated by
Benjamin Ivry
Stanford University Press, new edition
2016

*Rythme du temps, Astronomie et
calendriers,*
Émile Biémont
Éditions De Boeck & Larcier, Paris,
Bruxelles, 2000

*Dictionnaire de la civilisation
mésopotamienne,*
Edited by Francis Joannes
Robert Laffon, Paris, 2001

Calendar and Community,
Sacha Stern
Oxford University Press, 2001

*Les calendriers, leurs enjeux dans l'espace
et dans le temps,*
Colloque de Cerisy, 1-8 July
Jacques Le Goff, Jean Lefort, Perrine
Mane, Lise Andriès
Somogy éditions d'art, 2002

*Spheres, The Art of the Celestial
Mechanic*
J. Kugel, Paris 2002

*La Clepsydre, tome 2,
Entre Jérusalem et Babylone,
réappropriation du passé*
Sylvie-Anne Goldberg
Albin Michel, Paris, 2004

PHOTOGRAPHIC CREDITS

All photographs in this book are © Jean-Marc Breguet / Vacheron Constantin, with the exception of those on the following pages: 12, 13, 14, 15, 17, 18, 19, 20, 22, 23, 24, 25, 26, 28, 29, 31, 33, 35, 37 © Patrimoine Vacheron Constantin; 16 © Hulton Archives / Getty Archives; 21, 27 © Suddeutsche Zeitung / Rue des Archives; 38 © BNF Gallica; 41 © Flammarion / Giraudon / Bridgeman Images; 42-3 © RMN-Grand Palais (domaine de Chantilly) / René-Gabriel Ojéda; 45 © National Museum of History, Taipei, Taiwan, Dist. RMN-Grand Palais / image MNH; 46-7 © Universal History Archive/UIG / Bridgeman Images; 49 © Institute of Oriental Studies, St. Petersburg, Russia / Bridgeman Images ; 50-1 © Sotheby's; 53, 55 © YIVO, New York; 56 © BNF; 59 © Château de Versailles, Dist. RMN-Grand Palais / image château de Versailles; 60 © Musée d'Horlogerie du Locle, Château du Locle, Château des Monts, Switzerland; 63 © Archives Alinari, Florence, Dist. RMN-Grand Palais / Georges Tatge; 125 © Vacheron Constantin

ACKNOWLEDGEMENTS

Vacheron Constantin would like to express its warm gratitude to all those who have participated in the creation of this work, and especially to Fabienne-Xavière Sturm, Elisabeth Doerr, Richard Chadwick and Dominique Fléchon for their valuable contributions to the texts.